The Perennial Philosophy

Series

World Wisdom
The Library of Perennial Philosophy

The Library of Perennial Philosophy is dedicated to the exposition of the timeless Truth underlying the diverse religions. This Truth, often referred to as the *Sophia Perennis*— or Perennial Wisdom—finds its expression in the revealed Scriptures as well as in the writings of the great sages and the artistic creations of the traditional worlds.

What Does Islam Mean in Today's World: Religion, Politics, Spirituality appears as one of our selections in the Perennial Philosophy series.

The Perennial Philosophy Series

In the beginning of the twentieth century, a school of thought arose which has focused on the enunciation and explanation of the Perennial Philosophy. Deeply rooted in the sense of the sacred, the writings of its leading exponents establish an indispensable foundation for understanding the timeless Truth and spiritual practices which live in the heart of all religions. Some of these titles are companion volumes to the Treasures of the World's Religions series, which allows a comparison of the writings of the great sages of the past with the perennialist authors of our time.

OTHER WORKS
BY WILLIAM STODDART

Outline of Sufism: The Essentials of Islamic Spirituality

*What Do the Religions Say about Each Other? Christian
Attitudes towards Islam, Islamic Attitudes towards
Christianity*

*Invincible Wisdom: Quotations from the Scriptures, Saints,
and Sages of All Times and Places*

*Remembering in a World of Forgetting: Thoughts on
Tradition and Postmodernism*

Outline of Buddhism

Outline of Hinduism

What Does *Islam*
Mean in Today's World?

Religion, Politics, Spirituality

William Stoddart

Foreword by
Harry Oldmeadow

World Wisdom

What Does Islam Mean in Today's World:
Religion, Politics, Spirituality
©2012 World Wisdom, Inc.

Cover photo, "woman in mosque" © Sarah Casewit.
Used with permission.

Library of Congress Cataloging-in-Publication Data

Stoddart, William.
  What does Islam mean in today's world? : religion, politics,
spirituality / William Stoddart ; foreword by Harry Oldmea-
dow.
     p. cm. -- (The perennial philosophy series)
  Includes bibliographical references and index.
  ISBN 978-1-936597-14-7 (pbk. : alk. paper) 1. Islam--21st
century. 2. Islam--Essence, genius, nature. I. Oldmeadow,
Harry, 1947- II. Title.
  BP161.3.S76 2012
  297--dc23
                                              2012001473

Printed on acid-free paper in the United States of America

For information address World Wisdom, Inc.
P.O. Box 2682, Bloomington, Indiana 47402-2682
www.worldwisdom.com

Say: We believe in God and that which is revealed unto us, and that which is revealed unto Abraham and Ishmael and Isaac and Jacob and the tribes, and that which was given unto Moses and Jesus and the prophets from their Lord. We make no distinction between any of them, and unto Him we have submitted.

Koran, *Sūra* "Family of Imran", 3:84

O People of the Book! Ye have no faith until ye observe the Torah and the Gospel, and all that has been revealed unto you by your Lord.

Koran, *Sūra* "The Table", 5:68

*
* *

When ye see a cloud rise out of the west, ye say, There cometh a shower; and so it is. And when ye see the south wind blow, ye say, There will be heat; and it cometh to pass. Ye hypocrites, ye can discern the face of the sky and of the earth, but how is it that ye do not discern this time?

Luke 12:54-56

[*After speaking with the Roman Centurion*] Verily I say unto you, I have not found such great faith, no, not in Israel. And I say unto you that many shall come from the east and the west, and shall sit down with Abraham and Isaac and Jacob in the kingdom of Heaven. But the children of the kingdom shall be cast out into outer darkness: there shall be wailing and gnashing of teeth.

Matthew 8:10-11

How consoling it is for me to know that, all over the world, there are millions of people who, five times a day, bow down before God.

Pope Pius XII (1876-1958)

CONTENTS

ILLUSTRATIONS

FOREWORD

It is one of the most galling ironies of our times that the religious tradition which in many ways is best equipped to bring about a *rapprochement* of the world's religions, and thus contribute to a more harmonious world community, is often associated in the West with strife and discord, with terrorism and with the "clash of civilizations". Anyone seeking an answer to the urgent question posed in the title of the present volume must start with a recognition of three facts which do not sit comfortably together.

Firstly, Islam is a militant religion whose providential role is to recall a forgetful humanity to a constant remembrance of God. Given the times and the cyclic conditions in which we live, Islam must needs take up a combative and uncompromising position in confronting the many ills and evils of modernity. Not surprisingly this causes offense to those who worship the false idols which surround us on all sides and which betray an impoverished understanding of man's true vocation.

Secondly, much of what passes for "Islam" in the contemporary world is either a parody or a betrayal of the tradition's essential message and timeless values. That Islam's teachings and values have apparently been harnessed to much hatred and violence is a sad testimony to corruptions and degenerations within the Islamic world. (I need hardly add that aggressive religious xenophobia also finds shelter in the so-called fundamentalism of various stripes and colors within the worlds of Christianity and Judaism, and now even within parts of the East.) One of the most telling symptoms of the dark confusion within parts of the Islamic world is the overt hostility to Sufism, the mystical heart of Islam.

Thirdly, Islam in general and Sufism in particular have a special role to play in cultivating inter-religious concord and amity, not only because Islam belongs to both East and West, but by virtue of the fact that the descent of the Koran is the last in the great cycle of Revelations, and that, necessarily, at the heart of Islam there is a universal message about the mystical unity of all integral traditions. That message was most powerfully actualized within two of Islam's most radiant saints and sages, Muhyi'd-Dīn Ibn 'Arabī and Jalāl ad-Dīn Rūmī. Well-known to Sufis everywhere is the noble passage in which the *Shaikh al-Akbar* declares,

> My heart has opened unto every form; it is a pasture for gazelles, a cloister for Christian monks, a temple for idols, the Kaaba of the pilgrim, the tables of the Torah, and the book of the Koran. I practice the religion of Love; in whatsoever direction its caravans advance, the religion of Love shall be my religion and my faith (*Tarjumān al-Ashwāq*).

At a time when the outward and readily exaggerated incompatibility of divergent religious forms is used to exploit all manner of anti-religious prejudices, the affirmation of what Frithjof Schuon called "the transcendent unity of religions" can only be achieved by those who understand the *sophia perennis*, the immutable wisdom enshrined in all the great religious traditions of both East and West. It is only in its refulgent light that we can fully celebrate and cherish religious differences as well as affirm our common humanity under Heaven. Such an understanding does not vitiate, but rather strengthens, a commitment to traditional religious forms, and deepens our understanding of the precious and irreplaceable role played by each of the traditions in meeting the diverse spiritual needs of the human collectivity.

I have alluded to a few of the many vexed issues concerning the place of Islam in the modern world; these issues are illuminated in this small but percipient volume, which furnishes us with an informed and satisfying answer to the question, "What does Islam mean in today's world?" While the book focuses on one of the world's great spiritual treasures, it also has much to tell us about the nature of religion in general.

William Stoddart belongs in the Perennialist school most readily associated with such luminaries as René Guénon, Frithjof Schuon, Ananda Coomaraswamy, and Titus Burckhardt, a school devoted to the explication of unchanging metaphysical and cosmological principles and the preservation of the religious forms and institutions which give these principles concrete expression. I first met with Dr. Stoddart's work in *Sufism: The Mystical Doctrines and Methods of Islam* (1976),[1] and have since richly profited from his several works on Buddhism, Hinduism, the Perennial Philosophy, the manifold forms of Tradition, and the false ideologies of the contemporary world.

Amidst the confusions and perplexities of contemporary life, Dr. Stoddart has much to tell us. He has been a

[1] Recently republished in a revised and augmented edition as *Outline of Sufism: The Essentials of Islamic Spirituality* (Bloomington, IN: World Wisdom, 2012).

resolute defender of Tradition in all its forms and, by the same token, an implacable foe of the follies of modernity. We find in his books and essays a rare combination of metaphysical insight, a deep understanding of and sensitivity to religious forms, and a style of exposition and argumentation which is lucid, attractive, and accessible without ever sacrificing rigor or compromising the rights of Truth.

Harry Oldmeadow
La Trobe University Bendigo
Victoria, Australia
July 2011

INTRODUCTION

"Islam is the unknown religion." I first wrote these words in a book on Islamic spirituality published in 1976, and I see no need to change them now. For, not only is there still in the West a widespread ignorance of the true nature of Islam, there is also, thanks to the "Islamic" terrorists, a widespread hostility.

The cause of this hostility is not hard to understand, but it is nonetheless something of a paradox, given that two of the foremost Islamic mystics—who are the true and authentic voices of Islam—have for long been known and admired in the West: I refer to the Persian poets Rumi and Omar Khayyam. One might also mention another celebrated literary work that is familiar and much loved in the West, namely, the "Arabian Nights". Furthermore, in the field of Islamic architecture, there are the two marvels, the Alhambra at Granada in Spain and the Taj Mahal at Agra in India, which are amongst the best known and most admired buildings in the world.

These mystic poets and majestic sanctuaries are examples of an art that can truly be called sacred, for not only is its fundamental content spiritual, its very forms are in accordance with the canons of traditional art. Art has many branches, and the two sacred arts just mentioned, poetry and architecture, may be said to correspond respectively to verbal and visual crystallizations of the Divine Beauty.[1]

Religion, of course, is not only Beauty. It is first and foremost an expression of Truth and a provider of a means of Salvation. In these few words, we have reached the defining characteristics of every revealed religion: Truth, Beauty, and Salvation. In man, each of these fundamental pillars takes on a moral quality. Truth implies impartiality, rigorous objectivity, and a love of justice. Beauty, which includes Goodness and Mercy, evokes devotion, fervor, and gratitude. Salvation lies in prayer and the essential virtues of humility and charity.

To say the least, all of this is very far from the notion of Islam that exists in the public mind today. A true notion of Islam, and indeed of every complete and uncorrupted religion, is what the present book—taken in its entirety—is all about.

*
* *

This book deals with the nature of religion—Islamic and other—and how, in the present age, it has become subject to massive betrayal and perversion. It also touches on how religion is falsified by being amalgamated with secular political programs, which are superficial and outward in the extreme, and which are either entirely devoid of principles, or alternatively, imbued with fundamentally false principles.

---

[1] Analogous examples in Christianity of these two sacred arts would be Dante's *Divine Comedy* and the Medieval cathedrals. We should not forget the teaching of Plato: "Beauty is the splendor of the Truth." To which adage, Frithjof Schuon has added: "and Truth is the essence of Beauty".

CHAPTER 1

A SUCCESSION OF REVOLUTIONS: THE ASSAULTS ON RELIGION

Immediately following World War II (1939-1945), there was a natural feeling of relief that the carnage had ended. Although change of one kind or another was simmering beneath the surface, there was, nevertheless, a gradual return to "normal", and even, to some extent, to the life and values of the pre-war years; one could convince oneself that nothing had changed. But this period of relative calm, compounded as it was of a simple thankfulness and a modest optimism, lasted only a few years. From the fifties onwards, the first signs that a different future might lie ahead, began to appear.

Tell-tale pointers indicating that things were on the move started to crop up in all sorts of ways. One of the earliest manifestations was the "Beat Generation" of post-war American writers, who gravitated to California, and with whom were associated the "drug culture" and the "sexual revolution". Soon after that came the hippies who, with their "counter culture", continued along the same lines. Both movements involved some people of seriousness and good intentions—many turned to the teachings of the Eastern religions, especially Buddhism—but the overall effect was extremely negative. All these things coincided with the first beginnings of the fraudulent and immensely destructive "New Age" movement, the heir, so to speak, of the earlier Theosophical Society. Then there were "rock stars" on both sides of the Atlantic. The so-called music of the day was revolutionized, dress became more and more outlandish, and, in these same years, legislation was introduced to authorize the publication of what had previously been regarded as obscene literature. In a word, what had up to then been respected as societal norms and standards, now began to vanish.

The "Beat Generation" and the hippies did their bit, but the "revolutions" by no means stopped with them. Even more harmful and fundamental revolutions followed. Public, organized religion received deadly blows from both the Vatican II Council of 1962-1965 and the Iranian revolution fomented by Ayatollah Khomeini in 1979. The Vatican II Council directly concerned only Catholicism, but its relativizing, de-spiritualizing, and de-sacralizing spirit gradually, but inexorably, spread to the principal Protestant denominations, and even influenced the attitudes of the congregations (but not the dogmas and sacraments) of some of the Eastern Churches. The Iranian revolution directly affected only Shī'i Islam, but an ideology similar to that of Khomeini was also present in a slightly earlier revolution in Libya, namely the overthrow of King Idris of the Sanussi by Mu'ammar Gadhafi, and the establishment of a so-called "Islamic republic". Soon thereafter, these hollow, but evil, ideas gradually spread throughout the Islamic world. As for Catholicism, some Catholics at first resisted Vatican II, but very soon the majority welcomed it as a wonderful liberation from obscurantism, dogmatism, etc. As far as the West is concerned, Vatican II was the most destructive and harmful revolution of all.

It was in these same years that the rape of Tibet took place, and also that the gradual and deliberate dilution and weakening of Muslim society in East Turkestan (Sinkiang) began, both by the massive immigration of Han Chinese and by direct persecution. The 1960s and '70s were clearly the years of decisive and fundamental changes throughout the world; they constituted a significant "fall".

The arts and sciences certainly did not escape. Indeed the revolutions in these areas started much earlier: the nineteenth and twentieth centuries saw the appearance of the nefarious quintet: Darwin, Marx, Freud, Jung, and Teilhard de Chardin.[1] Although today their names are not so often mentioned, the influence of these destructive spirits permeates everywhere, and it is because of them that anything recognizable as "morality" began to vanish from the public domain; morality was gradually replaced by "political correctness". As for the influence of Teilhard de Chardin, it reached its apogee in the decrees of the Vatican II Council.

Darwin is generally reckoned to be the one who did the greatest damage to religion, although the last of them, Teilhard de Chardin, sums up in himself all the iniquities of the preceding four. Darwin's theory of evolutionism is a scientific hoax: it never took place! How can I say such a thing? Because there is not a shred of evidence for it. That it could not and did not happen has been

---

[1] One could make this a "nefarious sextet" by including the name of Einstein, whose theory of relativity, which officially applies only to mathematics and physics, quickly gave rise to the general belief that "all things are relative"—except, of course, this statement! Evolutionism and relativism effectively combine to exclude the absolute from contemporary thought.

demonstrated by many biologists, and it has led some of them, but unfortunately not all, to a belief in God. As for the public, most people simply yield to the "authority" of the scientists, the majority of whom avidly believe in evolution.

Many people mistake degeneration for evolution; they do not perceive the difference between them, although in fact they are opposites. The term "degeneration" is a reference to entropy, or the second law of thermodynamics: complexity tends to degradation; systems naturally move to a greater degree of randomness; without an input of "intelligence", order proceeds to disorder. This second law finds popular expression in the French saying: *Tout passe, tout casse, tout lasse* ("Everything passes away, everything breaks down, everything becomes tired").

As for the term "evolution", it can have a legitimate sense. It can mean the realization of a prototype or, in scholastic terms, the "passage from potency to act". Contemporary "evolutionism", however, is quite different: it quickly leads to "progressivism", the social consequences of which have been immense—and disastrous. It is not difficult to see that, far from "realizing a prototype" or a "norm", humanity has, for long, been falling away from one.

Just as in the sciences, so also in the arts, destructive forces were not lacking. These included: Picasso (in painting), Henry Moore (in sculpture), Le Corbusier (in architecture), Schoenberg (in music), James Joyce (in literature), and a host of others.[2]

---

[2] There is no single iconic name to attach to the equally destructive "feminist" movement, which seeks to make women the same as, or "equal" to, men, instead of making them "different" from men, which, however repugnant this may be to feminists, they already are! Spiritually speaking, of course,

A Succession of Revolutions: The Assaults on Religion

Some years after the hippies and Vatican II, there followed the "technology revolution", and finally the "electronic revolution", amidst the effects of which we now live. Then came "Islamic terrorism". This, coupled with the new technologies, engendered the age of universal surveillance.[3]

Some of these revolutions are discussed in greater detail elsewhere in this book.

Just as the majority of people in the West welcomed Vatican II, so many people in the Islamic world welcomed the Egyptian (1952), Libyan (1969), and Iranian (1979) revolutions (each one of which abolished the respective monarchy). This grim trend has been referred to as "the awakening of Islam", sometimes rashly and foolishly followed by the words: "after a long period of slumber". As Frithjof Schuon ominously remarked: "It is not Islam that is awakening!" What is it then? Roman Catholic Christians used to talk of the evil spirits who, "like a raging lion, wander through the world for the ruin of souls". Protestant Christians, until very recently, sang:

women are the equal of men—sometimes more so, sometimes less so depending on the individual. Certainly, there are always injustices to be righted, and this in all domains, including that of women but, perversely, "feminism" destroys femininity as well as masculinity. By the same token, it is lethal to the family, in which the two poles "father" and "mother" are indispensable. See Jane Casewit, "The Notion of Gender in the Light of Islamic Spirituality", *Sacred Web* 19, n.d. (Vancouver, British Columbia), pp. 145-170.

[3] I am not specifically discussing here communism or nazism, two of the most egregious evils of the twentieth century. I can only say that they possessed most of the faults of the modern world in general (and some of them to excess), in addition to their own particularly evil deeds and beliefs.

"Change and decay in all around I see. O Thou who changest not, abide with me." Not any more! Things have changed! Islam likewise warns us of the continuing decline; Mohammed said: "No time cometh upon you but is followed by a worse." Hinduism, with its doctrine of the Four Ages, the present one being the "Dark Age", tells the same story.[4]

All the world religions concur in warning us about what they call the "end times". It is only too clear what it is that is now "awakening"—and has been for some time. It is a revolutionary attitude of mind—narrow, superficial, and very aggressive—that is hostile to all authentic religion.

The scandal is not simply that terrible things have happened; it is that almost no one protests. The changes are radical and unprecedented, yet they have given rise to little concern on the part of an indifferent public; the public have other things to capture their attention: spectator sport, television, electronics, and an excessive preoccupation with physical fitness and mental health;[5] these things—without mentioning several egregious immoralities—fully occupy the minds of the majority. Little else seems to arouse the interest of contemporary people.

---

[4] The Hindu doctrine of the Four *Yugas* (*Satya, Treta, Dvapara, Kali*) corresponds to the Greco-Roman doctrine of the Four Ages, spoken of by Hesiod and Ovid, namely Golden, Silver, Bronze, and Iron. As noted above, the Hindus call the Iron Age the "Dark Age" (the *Kali-Yuga*).

[5] These words might cause misunderstanding: physical fitness and mental health are obviously both desirable. However, in today's world, concern for the much more important attribute of spiritual health, is conspicuous by its absence, and this leads to a tremendous disproportion, which is in no way attenuated by the prominence often given to pseudo-spirituality or pseudo-religion.

The above observations are extremely judgemental. Did not Christ say: "Judge not that ye be not judged" (Matt. 7:1)? As I stress later in this book, this is a text that is all too easily misinterpreted. It applies to our egoism, our subjectivism, our self-interest; it does not abolish objectivity, still less does it abolish justice or truth. There is manifestly plenty for us to "judge" and, having judged, to oppose, namely, atheism, agnosticism, and the various anti-traditional beliefs and attitudes that emerged from the eighteenth century Enlightenment and, two centuries later, from the revolutionary 1950s and '60s. Let us not forget that there is none so judgemental as the secular humanist. He judges everything. The trouble is that he judges wrongly—with devastating results for society.

Against all evidence, the secular humanist maintains that, through "science" and "reason",[6] religion will eventually wither away; but, although the religions have suffered grievously as a result of modern science, this is far from being the case. Religion, belief in God, is deeply rooted in the heart of man; it can never be extirpated completely. Nevertheless, it is not hard to see that religion also has a negative side, in that all of the great world religions are anchored in immense religious collectivities which, like all things under the sun, are subject to nature's inexorable law of "change and decay". These collectivities and their self-appointed leaders exploit religion, distort religion, and transform it into a superficial and aggressive/competitive "denominationalism". Though the eternal

---

[6] I have put these two items within quotation marks, for the science and reason envisaged by humanists have little to do with the *scientia* and *ratio* of Greco-Roman and Medieval philosophy. No doubt the essence of reason is the same in both cases, but in modern science, its operations are vitiated by being based on false or insufficiently complete premises.

message present in the heart of each religion can never be rubbed out, it is only too apparent that it can be pushed aside and forgotten.

In the West, the worst error of all is for Christians to equate Christianity with modern humanism, modern "progress", and modern "political correctness". This is nothing short of blasphemy; it is a fatal blindness which leads to what C. S. Lewis called "the abolition of man".

The aim of this book is to argue that traditional Christianity has today nothing to fear from traditional Islam. In spite of appearances, the two ancient religions are allies; they have common enemies; they are united in their opposition to all kinds of modern errors and immoralities. Leaving aside the question of terrorism (discussed later in this book), the main principle to be understood in this connection is that one religion cannot be judged by the criteria of another, and the main question to be asked is whether a given religion is true to itself, or whether, and to what extent, it has been perverted—or even invalidated entirely—by "the spirit of the times".

CHAPTER 2

THE URGENT NEED FOR UNBIASED
INFORMATION ABOUT ISLAM

Many periodicals and books today systematically present a highly biased and misleading picture of Islam. Amongst other things, it is often alleged that Islam is intolerant towards people of other faiths. The truth is that, amongst the religions of the world, Islam is unique as regards the high degree of tolerance which, throughout history, it has shown towards non-Muslim religions, in particular Christianity and Judaism. This is because tolerance of the "People of the Book" stems directly from the Koran and is encapsulated in Islamic law. Many will no doubt react to this statement with incredulity, but this will be enlarged upon, with many Koranic quotations, in the course of this chapter.

Islamic tolerance first showed itself with regard to Christianity. The Arab armies conquered many territories, and the first religion which they encountered was Christianity. In 635 A.D. the Muslims conquered Syria and Palestine. In 637 A.D., after a long siege, they entered the city of Jerusalem peacefully. The Patriarch,

Saint Sophronius, declared that he would sign no peace treaty with anyone other than the Caliph Omar himself. As a result, Omar traveled to Jerusalem with one servant and one mule—the servant and the Caliph took turns at walking and riding. When they reached the city, it was the servant's turn to ride, and the Caliph entered Jerusalem on foot. The Patriarch and the Caliph signed the "Covenant of Omar", the provisions of which are accepted by the native Christians and Muslims of Jerusalem to this day. When the Patriarch Sophronius invited Omar to pray in the Church of the Holy Sepulcher, he refused, on the grounds that, if he did so, his followers would wish to turn the church into a mosque.

For theological and historical reasons which I will not go into here, Jerusalem is in fact the third of the three quintessential Islamic cities: Mecca, Medina, and Jerusalem. Since this early conquest, Jerusalem has been under unbroken Muslim jurisdiction, with the exception of the 88-year period of crusader rule. The second Temple of Solomon was destroyed by the Romans, but the Church of the Holy Sepulcher, despite a checkered history, continues to flourish as a church to this day, and has been under the guardianship of generations of Muslim caretakers.

When the Arab armies reached India, there was indeed temple destruction and massacre. All that can be said here is that the Muslims in due course came to realize that the Hindus were not simply idolaters (like the pre-Islamic inhabitants of Arabia), but that they too, in their fashion, could by analogy be regarded as "People of the Book"; as a result, they were treated with tolerance in areas where Muslims ruled. Centuries later, under the great Mughals, there was an incredibly fruitful period of cultural and artistic interchange with the Hindu tradition, especially under Akbar (1542-1605) and Shah Jahan (1592-1666).

The latter's son, Dara Shikoh, declared: "The science of Vedanta and the science of Sufism are one." Dara Shikoh also had the *Bhagavad Gītā*, the *Yoga Vasīshtha*, and several of the *Upanishads* translated into Persian. Alas, the last of the great Mughals, the zealot Aurungzebe, reversed the tolerance of centuries. Nevertheless, the English historian Robert Lethbridge, in his book *A History of India*, says: "Amongst the courteous and order-loving natives of India religious disturbances are extremely rare. . . . The earnest and fearless way in which most Mussulmans rigorously attend to their devotional duties at the stated times is generally noticed [by Hindus] in their favor."[1]

The Arab armies never reached Indonesia, and yet this is the most populous Muslim country in the world. It was the Arab traders—and especially the Sufis amongst them—who converted Indonesia and the Malay peninsula to Islam.

One thinks also of the Mongols, who swept away all that was in their path, but who ended up by adopting the religion of the people they conquered.

In Yugoslavia, it was mainly the heretical Bogomil community which, during the period of Turkish rule, converted to Islam; today the Islamic community is to be found chiefly in Bosnia, where it constitutes the majority. The Serbs remained Orthodox and the Croats remained Catholic.

The falseness of the allegation that Islam was spread by the sword is decisively shown by the fact that the populations of Greece and Spain (both under Muslim rule for several centuries) remained Christian. The monastic community of Mount Athos in the North-East of Greece

---

[1] Robert Lethbridge, *A History of India* (London: Macmillan, 1881), pp. 127, 132.

flourished during the period that Greece was under Turkish rule but, as soon as the Turks were expelled from Greece, the monks of Mount Athos began to get grief from the modernistic and secularistic Greek government.

*

* *

It is constantly repeated that Islam was imposed by the sword. It was no doubt thus in the case of the idolatrous and treacherous tribes of ancient Arabia and elsewhere, but not in the case of Christians and Jews (apart from one case of egregious treachery by the latter at the beginning of Islam). The incredibly rapid expansion of the religion of Islam was due above all to persuasion, example, and especially to its inherent power of attraction, its Divine irresistibility. Here are some quotations from the writings of historians:

> Force had no part in the propagation of the Koran, for the Arabs always left those they conquered to keep their religion. . . . Far from being imposed by force, the Koran was spread only by persuasion. Persuasion alone could induce peoples who conquered the Arabs at a later date, such as the Turks and the Mongols, to adopt it.[2]
>
> (Gustave Le Bon, *La Civilisation des Arabes* [*The Civilization of the Arabs*])

> Of any organized attempt to force the acceptance of Islam on the non-Muslim population, or of any systematic persecution to stamp out the Christian religion, we hear nothing. Had the early Caliphs

---

[2] Paris: Firmin-Didot, 1884.

12

chosen to adopt either course of action, they might have swept away Christianity as easily as Ferdinand and Isabella drove Islam out of Spain.
(Thomas W. Arnold,[3] *The Preaching of Islam: A History of the Propagation of the Muslim Faith*)[4]

We see Muslim and Catholic princes not only allied, when the power of a dangerous co-religionist had to be curbed, but also aiding one another generously to suppress disorders and revolts. The reader will learn, no doubt to his surprise, that in one of the battles for the Caliphate of Córdoba in 1010 Catalan forces saved the situation, and on this occasion three bishops gave their lives for the "Prince of the Believers" (*amīr al-mu'minīn*). Al-Mansūr had in his entourage several counts who joined him with their troops, and the presence of Christian guards in the courts of Andalusia was by no means exceptional."
(Ernst Kühnel, *Maurische Kunst [Moorish Art]*)[5]

In Muslim Spain, those who remained Christian were well treated, as they were throughout the Islamic Empire. Both Jews and Christians were regarded as "People of the Book", that is, as people who had their own holy writings, the Old and the New Testaments of the Bible. In Córdoba, the Christians continued to worship in the Cathedral of Saint Vincent, though they were not allowed

---

[3] A nineteenth century Protestant missionary.

[4] Westminster: A. Constable & Co., 1896.

[5] Berlin: Cassirer, 1924.

to disturb the Muslims with hymn-singing or bell-ringing.

Muslims and Christians usually got on very well together, lived much the same life, and dressed alike. Muslims took pleasure in attending Christian celebrations and were frequent visitors at monasteries on saints' days. Even warfare did not divide them. Christians in Muslim Spain were loyal to the emir and fought for their Muslim ruler against the Christian kings of the north. In peacetime Christian kings sent their sons to be taught manners at the court of Córdoba. They married their daughters to Muslim princes and these brides became Muslims too.

Arabic language and literature fascinated Spanish Christians, as did Muslim architecture and science. A Christian of Córdoba named Álvaro wrote in 854: "Innumerable are the Christians who can express themselves in Arabic and compose poetry in that language with greater art than the Arabs themselves."

A popular recreation for rich and poor alike was getting together for picnics and garden parties. People in Córdoba had a passion for them and any occasion would do. Marriages and circumcisions—all Muslim boys were circumcised—called for splendid celebrations. Then there were the Muslim and Christian feast days. At the Christian feast of the Epiphany the whole population joined in the torch-lit processions that went on all night. There were saint's day pilgrimages to Christian monasteries where the monks gave lavish hospitality. . . . The feast days were great occasions."

(Duncan Townson, *Muslim Spain*)[6]

---

[6] Cambridge, UK: Cambridge University Press, 1973.

*
* *

In my opening paragraph, I said that, amongst the world religions, Islam is unique as regards the degree of tolerance which, throughout history, it has shown towards non-Muslim religions, especially Christianity and Judaism. Some evidence to this effect has been given above; but now I will change tack.

It is said that two wrongs don't make a right. How true! Nevertheless, two wrongs—indeed many wrongs—immediately remove the allegedly *unique* nature of the "wrongness" commonly attributed to Islam.

As regards intolerance and violence, how does Christianity shape up? Shall we start with the Inquisition, the cruel burning at the stake of untold numbers of heretics, the marauding crusaders, the wars of religion, the aggression against Eastern Orthodoxy by Catholics, against Catholics by Protestants, against Jews by Orthodox, Catholics, and Protestants alike?

Albert the Great, Saint Thomas Aquinas, Martin Luther, and many others amongst the great Christian figures in history, spoke extremely negatively about the Jews; and so, for that matter, does the New Testament (in both the Gospels and the Apocalypse). Islamic lore also contains examples of similar attitudes and statements. In both religions, the fundamental reason for this is theological, namely the Jews' rejection of the Messiah.

There is much talk nowadays along the lines of: "*Their* God ('Allah') is vengeful; *our* God ('Jehovah') is merciful." One would like to refer people who speak thus to the Koran and the Bible, for they are clearly ignorant of both. I will quote from the Koran later, but as regards the Bible, see Exodus 22:20; 32:26-28; Deuteronomy 7:2; 13:15-16; 20:13; 20:16-17; 22:20-21; 28:23-26; 32:41-42; Joshua 10:40; Judges 21:10. Merciless massacres, and exterminations of whole tribes, were commanded by God. In a divinely sanctioned act, Samson killed himself and three thousand people with him (Judges 16:25-30; Mark 6:11; Jude 5). Jesus himself exhibited anger on many occasions, and spoke repeatedly of hellfire.

Perhaps at this point I need to say the obvious: there is only one God, whatever He may be called! The Arabic word for God is "Allah". Protestants in particular seem to be unaware that Christians all over the Near-East refer to God as "Allah".

Saladin's career is known in detail. It is through this, that he acquired his reputation for exemplary chivalry, a reputation which has lasted from his own time to the present. Sir Walter Scott, for example, eulogizes him in his novel *The Talisman*.

When one surveys comprehensively and objectively the whole historical scene, one can soon observe that the Muslim record regarding non-Muslim populations is manifestly better than that of Christians in analogous situations. One example from the Middle Ages: when in 1097, during the first crusade (1095-1099), the crusaders captured Jerusalem, they indiscriminately killed *all* of its inhabitants, men, women, and children; Muslims, Jews, and the large population of non-Catholic Christians. It was said that the city was knee-high in blood.

After ninety years of crusader rule, the Muslims, under the command of Saladin, re-captured Jerusalem in 1187, following the fierce and bloody battle of Hattin, a battle to the death if there ever was one. Two crusader leaders were captured: Guy de Lusignon and Raynald de Châtillon. In this connection, Saladin declared: "It is not the wont of kings to kill kings." Accordingly, the life of Guy was spared, but Raynald de Châtillon was executed, because he had earlier attacked and killed a group of unarmed Muslim pilgrims on their way to Mecca.

After the battle, according to the historian Bahā ad-Dīn Shaddād,[7] Saladin ordered the execution of every single member of the military monastic orders that had fought against the Muslims (except for the Grand Master of the Temple); it is further said that this execution of the Knights Templars and Hospitallers was carried out by Sufis. May be; but this is completely foreign to Sufis and Sufism as known throughout the ages, and as attested to by the three unimpeachable authorities on Sufism, Reynold Nicholson, Arthur Arberry, and Annemarie Schimmel.[8]

Dismaying as the execution of the members of the military monastic orders is (if the account is true, it was spiritual men killing spiritual men), it may be that it harbors an underlying symbolic and poetic justice, which would differentiate it sharply from the insensate massacres, in modern times, of twenty million Christians by Stalin, twenty million Buddhists by Mao, and six million Jews by Hitler.[9] In connection with Saladin's action, it may also be appropriate to recall that, in several books of the Bible, as also in the Koran, God commanded the massacre of individuals, groups, and whole tribes.

Quite other, and more positively symbolic, is the fact that, when Saladin's troops entered Jerusalem, *no one*, were he Catholic, Eastern Christian, or Jew, was killed.

---

[7] His laudatory biography of Saladin, of whom he was a personal friend, bears the quaint title *Sultanly Anecdotes and Josephly Virtues*. The English translation, under the title *The Rare and Excellent History of Saladin* is still in print.

[8] I comment on this more fully in my book *What do the Religions say about Each Other? Christian Attitudes towards Islam, Islamic Attitudes towards Christianity* (San Rafael, CA: Sophia Perennis, 2008).

[9] The number killed after Hattin was around 230.

The Catholics, indeed, were given a free passage out of the city. The Eastern Christians and the Jews remained.

Soon after Ferdinand and Isabella completed the *reconquista* in 1492 by capturing the remaining Muslim province of Granada, the Muslims and Jews there were either expelled or forcibly converted. Cardinal Richelieu in Paris later declared that these persecutions and expulsions, which involved horrendous cruelty, were amongst the most barbarous actions ever recorded in human history.

The Spanish in South and Central America and the Americans (i.e. the British) in North America were scarcely paragons of Gandhian non-violence. Nevertheless, the indigenous people who became Christians were generally pious. I have heard it said that in their Indian colony of Goa, the Portuguese solved the annoying problem of religious plurality by massacring the Muslims and forcibly converting the Hindus! The Spaniards imposed Christianity in the Philippines.[10]

As for the Hindus: from the seventh to eleventh centuries, they subjected Buddhists to severe persecution. Because of this persecution, and also because of a resurgence of Hinduism, Buddhism was almost completely driven out of India.

Anyone familiar with the blood-stained histories of China, Japan, and Tibet can see how readily Buddhists ignored and pushed aside the tenets of their allegedly "peaceful" religion.

As for the Red Man: the tribes were ceaselessly on the warpath and engaged in much cruelty.[11]

---

[10] In all fairness, it must be said that the Goans and the Filipinos became devoted and pious Catholics.

[11] It is right to oppose the role played by missionaries but, with regard to Red Indian cruelty, Frithjof Schuon has said that

To end this section, let me make the important point that the modern "Christian" toleration of non-Christian religions is almost entirely due to indifference: the fact that nowadays the overwhelming majority of people in the West do not take religion seriously. Christianity has been *de facto* replaced by humanism. As indicated above, when Christianity was taken seriously—or when it was in a position of power—the situation was quite different. Today's much vaunted "freedom of religion" does not come from Christianity, but from modern humanism and religious indifference. On the contrary, Christianity (like every other authentic religion) spurns the alleged benefits of humanism, and asks, in the words of Christ, "What does it profit a man if he gain the whole world, and lose his own soul?" (Matt. 16:26).

As regards the question of cruel punishments, this was by no means exclusive to Islam: it was absolutely universal. In the Old Testament, for example, it is repeatedly ordained that adultery be punished by stoning, and on one occasion, it ordains burning. Without giving any further examples—

the Indians *needed* Christ (if not the missionaries!); and that it was through Christ that they renounced this form of savagery—without of course renouncing the religion of the Sun Dance and the Sacred Pipe (See Frithjof Schuon, *The Feathered Sun* [Bloomington, IN: World Wisdom, 1991], p. 42). How could the Indians learn about Christ without the missionaries? They did learn about Christ from the missionaries, but the missionaries' intention was to obtain total and exclusive "conversion" to the denomination concerned, and total extirpation of the indigenous religion and languages. Also, the missionaries and the civil authorities treated the Indians and their children most cruelly. However, the missionaries were not the only Christian presence; there were often honest White farmers nearby. These people would sometimes bring their sick children and other relatives to the last day of the Sun Dance to be healed by the leader of the Sun Dance and by the spiritual power of the Sacred Lodge.

this would be an altogether too horrifying exercise—it is enough to record that cruel punishments were present in *every* religious civilization. In Christianity, there have been terrible examples right up to the eighteenth century, if indeed not beyond. At the doctrinal level, we may note that the traditional Catholic prayer of contrition refers the need to avoid "God's dreadful punishments".

I refrain from speaking at length of the unspeakable present age. As far as it is concerned, we have little alternative but to be resigned; we know that whatever happens in these end times happens because it is the will of God. "There must needs be scandal" (Matt. 18.7).

*
* *

And what about Islam's oppression of women? Let us first look at the Bible:

> And the Lord God said unto the woman: Thy desire shall be to thy husband, and he shall rule over thee.
>
> Gen. 3:16

> The head of every man is Christ; and the head of the woman is the man; and the head of Christ is God. . . . Man is the image and glory of God, but the woman is the glory of man. Neither was the man created for the woman, but the woman for the man.
>
> I Cor. 11:3, 7-9

> Wives submit yourselves unto your own husbands as to the Lord. For the husband is the head of the wife, even as Christ is the head of the church.

Therefore as the church is subject unto Christ, so let the wives be to their own husbands in every thing.

Eph. 5:22-24

Let your women keep silence in the churches: for it is not permitted unto them to speak: but they are commanded to be under obedience, as also saith the law. And if they will learn anything, let them ask their husbands at home: for it is a shame for women to speak in the church.

I Cor. 14:34-35

I will therefore that women adorn themselves in modest apparel. . . . Let the woman learn in silence with all subjection. I suffer not a woman to teach, nor to usurp authority over the man, but to be in silence. For Adam was first formed and then Eve. Nevertheless, she shall be saved in childbearing, if they continue in faith and charity and holiness with sobriety.

I Tim. 2:8, 11-15

It is only fair to add that both traditional Judaism and traditional Christianity accorded a noble and sacred role to women.

Before terminating this list of traditional Western attitudes towards women, we may also recall the words of Aristotle: "As to the indulging of women in any particular liberties, it is hurtful to the end of government and the prosperity of the city" (*Politics*, Bk. 2, Chap. IX, 1269b12).

What then is Islam's attitude towards women? Are we going to say that the attitude of Islam is "better" (less rigorous) than the Biblical and Aristotelian ones? No; that would not be true. It may well be that, in the many

Islamic countries between Morocco and Indonesia, the situation is similar—slightly "less rigorous" in some cases, slightly "more rigorous" in others. (I am still referring to a comparison with the Biblical attitude, not with that of Europe since the Enlightenment.) As far as Morocco is concerned, it seems that the situation of the Berber women in the Atlas region is less rigorous and less formalistic than that of the Arab women. (I have to say however that I have seen, and met, what I must call "happy and contented" women in Arab areas of Morocco.) The Berber women in Chaouen in the Rif region, swathed in white, glide through the town like angels![12] A similar freedom for women can be seen among the Bedouin people, where women enjoy a good status. One can also note that the Muslim women of Black Africa (both East and West), in their proud demeanor and colorful—and not particularly puritan—costumes, seem to enjoy a status somewhat different from that of women in other Islamic countries.

Let me now turn directly to the shame and horror of a degenerate and perverted Islam. I refer to the abominable plight of women in a certain sector of Islam notoriously characterized by Afghanistan and similar areas. Here the servitude and indignity inflicted on women is egregious. A particularly apparent aspect of this oppression is the grotesque form of dress which women are constrained to wear—a dress which covers them in black from head to foot, with only a slit for the eyes. The sheer ugliness of this attire indicates only too clearly the degree of the deviation concerned. All this may be part of the world of Islam— Islam in a particularly aberrant and distorted form—but it is not the crystalline world of mercy and beauty that is

---

[12] I speak of Morocco as it was on my visits there in the 1950s and 1960s. I don't doubt that it has changed much since then.

the world of the Koran and the world of Mohammed.[13] Unhappily, because of the malignant growth of "Islamic fundamentalism" in recent times, this deformed Islam is now in a position to menace each and every country in the Islamic world. Frithjof Schuon has observed how this fundamentalism "monstrously combines Muslim formalism with modernist ideologies and tendencies".[14] One can think, for example, of Khomeini's "Islamic revolution" in Iran and Gadhafi's "Islamic republic" in Libya. Examples of enlightened Islamic civilization may be found in Moorish Spain (particularly under Abd ar-Rahman III and other Umayyads) and in Mughal India (particularly under Akbar and others amongst the great Mughals). In these two lands, there was not only splendor in the arts, there were also peaks of wisdom and piety. There were saints and philosophers in both countries. One can mention in particular Ibn 'Arabī in Spain and Mu'īn ad-Dīn Chishtī in India.

Regarding the principles and ideals of the Islamic attitude towards women, one may cite the following passages from Frithjof Schuon:

> The genesis of a religion amounts to the creation of a new moral and spiritual type; in Islam, this type consists in the equilibrium between

---

[13] Speaking thus of Mohammed may elicit the objection: "but Mohammed was at war nearly all the time." Yes, and so was the author of the Psalms; one might wonder if King David ever spent more than a moment in his palace in Jerusalem. The fact is that David and Mohammed were both engaged in the "lesser", as well as the "greater", holy war. See pp. 39-40.

[14] Frithjof Schuon, *In the Face of the Absolute* (Bloomington, IN: World Wisdom, 1989), p. 228.

contemplativeness and combativeness, and between holy poverty and sanctified sexuality. The Arab—and the man Arabized by Islam—has, so to speak, four poles: the desert, the sword, woman, and religion. For the contemplative, these poles become inward: the desert, the sword, and woman become so many states or functions of the soul. . . .

The sword represents death, the death one deals and the death one risks; its perfume is always present. Woman represents an analogous reciprocity; she is the love one receives and the love one gives, and thus she incarnates all the generous virtues; she compensates for the perfume of death with that of life. The profoundest meaning of the sword is that there is no nobility without a renunciation of life. . . . The symbiosis of love and death, within the framework of poverty and in the face of the Absolute, constitutes all that is essential in Arab nobility. . . .[15]

The Saracens renounced the conquest of Toledo because the queen of this city appeared on the ramparts to tell the assailants that her husband the king was absent. In this case, chivalric honor also enters into play; one does not wish to

---

[15] As regards the pole "death", it is similar in Christianity: here death is present in three forms: the knight or warrior who is ready to kill or be killed for the sake of truth or honor; the monk who renounces the lay life and his individual freedom by taking the monastic vow of "poverty, chastity, and obedience"; and, above all, the martyr, who eagerly seeks martyrdom, and willingly dies for Christ. Christ said: "He that loses his life for my sake, shall find it" (Matt. 16:25) and also: "I came not to bring peace, but a sword" (Matt. 10:34).

proceed against a frail woman, even though she be surrounded by warriors.[16]

Rumi observes, with finesse and profundity, and not without humor, that the sage is conquered by woman, whereas the fool conquers her; for the latter is brutalized by his passion and knows neither the *baraka* [spiritual blessing] of love nor delicate sentiments, whereas the sage sees in the lovable woman a ray from God, and in the feminine body an image of creative power.[17]

In view of its veneration for the Virgin Mary ("the Immaculate Conception"), and from the time of Khadija, Fatima, and Ayesha[18] onwards, Islam accords an honorable and sacred role to women. There is more in the Koran about the Virgin Mary than in the New Testament. One of the chapters in the Koran is named after her.

Mohammed's view of motherhood is revealed in the following incident:

A man asked Mohammed: "O Messenger of God, who has the greatest right to my companionship in good spirit?" Mohammed replied: "Thy mother." The man asked again: "Then who?" He answered: "Thy mother." Again the man asked: "Then who?" He answered: Thy mother." Once

---

[16] *Christianity/Islam: Perspectives on Esoteric Ecumenism* (Bloomington, IN: World Wisdom, 2007), pp. 115, 117.

[17] *Sufism: Veil and Quintessence* (Bloomington, IN: World Wisdom, 2006), p. 53n.

[18] Khadija and Ayesha were wives of Mohammed, and Fatima was his daughter.

more he asked: "Then who?" Mohammed said: "Thy father."

Christians are disconcerted by the fact that Mohammed had eleven wives. This offends their sensibility because the Christian sacrament of Holy Matrimony envisages only the union of "one man and one woman".[19] By way of explanation, one must again have recourse to the Bible and the Hebrew prophets. David, Solomon, and others amongst the prophets, had a very large number of wives, while remaining entirely within the will of God (despite the denials of this last point by many Evangelical preachers). Christianity, situated historically between Judaism and Islam, is the exception in the Semitic cycle. At any rate, it is a fact that the polygamy of the Hebrew prophets does not unduly trouble the majority of Christians. Analogously to "double standards", one could perhaps speak here of "double sensibilities".

In the wake, therefore, of this long-standing Semitic tradition, Muslims too are allowed multiple wives—in their case up to four (though, in fact, very few of them have more than one). According to Islamic teaching, Mohammed, for political, religious, and personal reasons, received divine authority to exceed this number.

*
*   *

The dreadful events and developments of the last few years have caused the Western public to ask, more or less for the first time: what kind of religion is Islam? Those good people who seek conciliation reply that Islam is

---

[19] I will not comment on the blasphemies and immoralities of the age we live in.

"a religion of peace".[20] Well, yes, and so is every other religion, although we must not forget that Christ said: "I came not to bring peace but a sword" (Matt. 10:34)—and that a principle analogous to this is also present in every religion.

Much more importantly, every religion claims to be, first and foremost, "a religion of truth". In the words of Christ, it is truth that "sets you free" (John 8:32). Thus every religion makes the dual claim to be a vehicle of truth, and a provider of a means of salvation. Were it not so, it would not be a religion, but a man-made ideology, with no ability to save anyone. Truth and a means of salvation are the defining characteristics of a religion.

Islam is characterized by what are called the "five pillars". These are: faith, prayer, fasting, almsgiving, and pilgrimage. Faith (*īmān*) that "there is no god but God"; prayer (*salāt*) five times a day; fasting (*saum*) during the holy month of Ramadan; almsgiving (*zakāt*) "to the poor, the widows, and the orphans"; and pilgrimage (*hajj*)—once in a life-time, if it is possible—to the Abrahamic "black stone" in the Kaaba in Mecca. As is well known, *jihād* (holy war) is also an important feature. According to Mohammed, the fight against idolaters is the "lesser holy war"; the fight against our own souls is the "greater holy war". This is the teaching of every religion. In Christianity, for example, it is known as the "spiritual combat"

[20] Islam is pre-eminently a "religion of peace". The very name indicates this: *islām* (resignation to the will of God) engenders *salām* (peace). The universal greeting of Islam is *salām* (peace). "Fight in the way of God against those who fight against you, but begin not hostilities. Verily God loveth not aggressors" (Koran, *Sūra* "The Cow", 2:190).

Islam is also a religion of mercy: every chapter of the Koran except one begins with the words: "In the Name of God the Clement, the Merciful".

(Lorenzo Scupoli) or "unseen warfare" (the *Philokalia*). In Hinduism, it is the battlefield of Kurukshetra (as described in the *Bhagavad Gītā*).[21]

*
* *

Muslim zealots are no better than Christian zealots. The latter, throughout the centuries and down to the present day, are to be found in all of the three great Christian sectors: Eastern Orthodoxy (the Serbs against Croatia, Bosnia, and Kosovo; the persisting spirit of "EOKA" [the Greek Cypriot terrorist organization] or *enosis* [the desired union of Cyprus with Greece] against the Turks in Cyprus); Roman Catholicism (the Crusader sacking of Constantinople, the massive killing of Eastern Christians by the Crusaders, the massacre of Saint Bartholomew's Day in France, the IRA in Northern Ireland); and Protestantism (the fanatical and violent element amongst the "Covenanters", the cruel witch hunting, the Protestant terrorists in Northern Ireland, and the attitude of many of the "religious right" in the United States).

It is often emphasized that the Islamic terrorists are anti-Christian. This is indeed the case; but what is not so tirelessly reiterated is that these evil men's mayhem is also directed against fellow-Muslims. They indeed are the first victims. There have been many lethal attacks by Islamic terrorists in Indonesia, Morocco, Jordan, Pakistan, Turkey, Iraq, Afghanistan, and other Muslim countries. It would be far from the truth to say that the terrorism in Muslim countries is only directed against tourists. It is directed against all Muslims who fail to adopt the terrorist ideology and who remain faithful to the traditional religion of

---

[21] For another reference to the difference in structure between Christianity and Islam, see p. 55.

Islam; all such people are potential targets. In this way the terrorists have caused widespread intimidation. In the case of Iraq the violence has been between opposing sects.

The media of publicity frequently and rightly draw attention to the sufferings of the people of Darfur in Sudan, but it is seldom mentioned that these hapless victims of a malevolent government are Muslims.

Many Orientals of all religions have a distaste for the manifest and grotesque decadence of Western "culture" and mores; but Arabs and other Muslims have an additional ground for complaint. I refer to the fact that, during the twentieth century, the Islamic world was subjected to certain major injustices of which the majority of people in the West are not even aware. It is precisely this unawareness that is the cause of such pain and bitterness throughout the populations of the Muslim world. An analogy: though the world was uncaring and indifferent, all Germans were aware of the fundamental injustices of the Treaty of Versailles, but this did not make them responsible for the misdeeds of Hitler, who was able to exploit this awareness for his own evil ends. In like manner, the Muslim peoples are aware of the injustices referred to, but are not thereby responsible for the actions of the terrorists.

In the face of man's callous injustice—not excusable simply because it is often unconscious—one can obtain profound solace in the words of Longfellow: "The mills of God grind slowly, yet they grind exceeding small." The Romans said that "Truth is the daughter of time" (*Veritas filia temporis*) and, according to an ancient English proverb: "Truth will out."[22] If the perpetrators of injustice knew what these sayings mean, it would send shivers up and down their spine!

---

[22] See also 1 Esdras 4:41, quoted on p. 34.

As for "Islamic terrorists", it is they, seeking bloody revenge and imbued with ideological fundamentalism, who are both the cause and the perpetuation of the regrettable "Islamophobia" which is now widespread in the West. That the Western public conflates terrorism and Islam is the lamentable achievement of the "Islamic terrorists".

It is frequently alleged that Islam wants to convert the whole world to Islam. The reader, who has got this far in my discourse, may be surprised when I unhesitatingly concur! For this is indeed the case, and I can say it without a qualm, because it is exactly the same with Christianity and Buddhism. Unlike Hinduism and Judaism (each one being "the religion of a people", and seeking no converts), Buddhism, Christianity, and Islam are "universal religions" (each one seeking converts in all nations); it is thus quite inevitable that there be competition between them. Nevertheless, each of these three religions is in fact located chiefly in a particular area of the world which, in a sense, has become its providential home. Buddhism originated in India, but virtually disappeared from that country, and took root in Tibet, China, Japan, and many other countries of South-East Asia. Christianity originated in a Jewish context, but took root principally amongst the Greeks, Romans, Germanics, Celts, and Slavs. Islam originated in Arabia, but, beyond the Arab world, it spread to Turkey, Persia, a portion of India, Malaysia, and Indonesia.

That this territorial distribution is not entirely a matter of chance is strongly suggested by the fact that the empire of Julius Caesar became, largely, the cradle for Christianity, and the empire of Alexander became, largely, the cradle for Islam. Caesar is mentioned in the Gospels, and Alexander is mentioned in the Koran.

Here are two Koranic verses which make specific reference to the plurality of religions:

O Mankind! We created you from a single pair, a male and a female, and made you into nations and tribes so that ye may know each other (not that ye may despise each other).

Sūra "The Apartments", 49:13

Had God willed, He would have made you a single community, but He wanted to test you by that which He has given you. So compete with one another in good works. Every one of you will return to God and He will inform you about the things wherein you differed.

Sūra "The Table", 5:48

*
* *

The choice of Koranic verses and sayings of Mohammed that are quoted in the hostile books and articles published today are carefully selected so as to include everything and anything that can be given a negative interpretation; they bypass the numerous and unmistakably clear expressions of Islamic tolerance, such as the following:

You will find that the best friends of believers [i.e. Muslims] are those who say: "We are Christians." This is because there are priests and monks amongst them, and because they are not proud.

Sūra "The Table", 5:82

O People of the Book! Ye have no faith until ye observe the Torah and the Gospel, and all that has been revealed unto you by your Lord.

Sūra "The Table", 5:68

O People of the Book! Come now to a word common to us and you, so that we worship none but God.

Sūra "The Family of Imran", 3:64

Verily, those who believe [i.e. Muslims], those who are Jews, Sabeans, and Christians, and whosoever believeth in the Last Day and doeth good: no fear shall come upon them, neither shall they grieve.

Sūra "The Table", 5:69

Were it not that God had repelled some men by means of others, monasteries and churches and synagogues and mosques, wherein the name of God is invoked, would assuredly have been destroyed.[23]

Sūra "The Pilgrimage", 22:40

Every son of Adam at birth is touched by Satan, save only the son of Mary and his mother.

Hadīth

If anyone testifies that there is no god but God, who alone has no partner, that Mohammed is His servant and messenger, that Jesus is His servant and messenger, the son of His handmaid, His Word which He cast into Mary and a Spirit from Him, and that Paradise and hell are real, then God will cause him to enter Paradise no matter what he has done.

Hadīth

---

[23] This translation is based on the English version of the Koran by Muhammad Asad. Elsewhere preference has generally been given to Marmaduke Pickthall's translation.

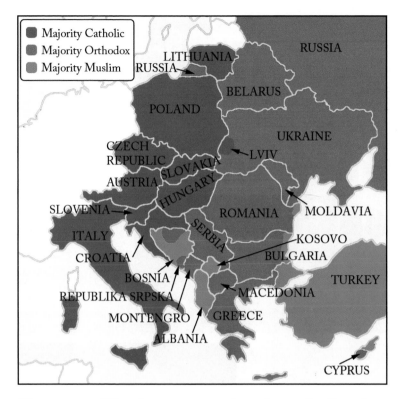

The country of Yugoslavia was created—rather artificially, as later became obvious—on the downfall of the Austro-Hungarian and Ottoman empires after World War I. Following the brutal internal wars of the 1990s, Yugoslavia broke into seven independent countries: three majority *Eastern Orthodox*: Serbia, Macedonia and Montenegro; two majority *Roman Catholic*: Croatia and Slovenia; and two majority *Muslim*: Bosnia and Kosovo. The "Republika Srpska", with a chiefly Serbian (*Eastern Orthodox*) population, is composed of northern and eastern enclaves within the territory of Bosnia, and enjoys self-government. Albania, lying between Bosnia and Greece, was never a part of Yugoslavia and is a separate *Muslim* country.

The island of Cyprus is divided between the Greek west and south (*Orthodox*) and the Turkish east and north (*Muslim*).

In Lviv and other Western parts of Ukraine, the *Uniat Eastern Church* predominates; it follows the Eastern rite (the same as that of the Orthodox), but is titularly under Rome.

I

The Kaaba at Mecca

The Prophet's Mosque
at Medina

II

> Whosoever cheats a non-Muslim citizen, or usurps his possessions, I shall be his prosecutor on the Day of Judgement.
>
> *Hadīth*

On the basis of these fundamental Islamic criteria, it can be said, without wasting words, that the so-called "Islamic terrorists" are not Muslims, just as, on the basis of the Catechism of the Council of Trent, it can be said that the five post-Vatican-II "popes" are not Catholics. It might well be asked: if this be true, why don't either ordinary Muslims or the Islamic authorities speak up and condemn terrorism? The systematically overlooked fact is that many of them have done and continue to do so. On the other hand, it must also be said that in most countries the terrorists have succeeded overwhelmingly in intimidating the Islamic community. In such a situation it is only human nature to keep silent.

*
* *

The calumnies of the contemporary media are based on pre-existing prejudice and systematic bad will. Authors of defamations of this sort appear to have no concern for truth and absolutely no awareness that they are dealing with one of the great religions of the world.

Apocalyptic Note

In this connection, it must not be overlooked that we are living in the end times. The Hindus say that we have been in the *Kali-Yuga* (the "Dark Age")[24] for millennia.

---

[24] For details regarding the "Four Ages" of Hinduism, see p. 6, fn. 4.

The whole of the *Kali-Yuga* is an age of lies, violence, and cruelty, and now more so than ever, since we appear to be in its last phases.

Everyone knows that war is hell. In war, combatants have never treated one another very nicely. In the past, people fought with ancient weapons; now with mechanized slaughter and indiscriminate destruction from the air; but, in the "dark age", wars will always occur. People fight for causes good or bad; angelic or demonic; for causes supported with truth or with lies; for causes made plain or for causes kept hidden. But one thing is certain: when people rush to judgement on these matters, double standards immediately and shamelessly come into play.

We know that, in these days, the evil one has free rein. He has dealt well-nigh death-blows to all the religions: The Vatican II Council and the Islamic "fundamentalism" are two examples, but the other religions have, in one form or another, undergone analogous injury.

It is sometimes hard to believe the verse: *Magna est veritas et praevalebit* ("Truth is great and it shall prevail." I Esdras 4:41). But, despite an unremitting barrage of mendacious propaganda and apparently endless killing, it is true.

One can take solace in the verse: "Heaven and earth will pass away, but My words will not pass away" (Matt. 24:35). These apocalyptic words of Christ apply *mutatis mutandis* within all of the great religions.

An understanding of what the end times involve is an important key to understanding the past and present misdeeds of religion.

The Dome of the Rock at Jerusalem

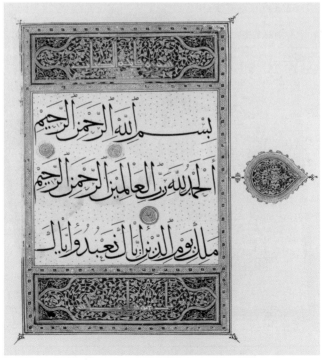

Koran: *Al-Fātiha*, "The Opening *Sūra*"

III

Saint Catherine's Monastery at Mount Sinai.
The monastery that contains a mosque.

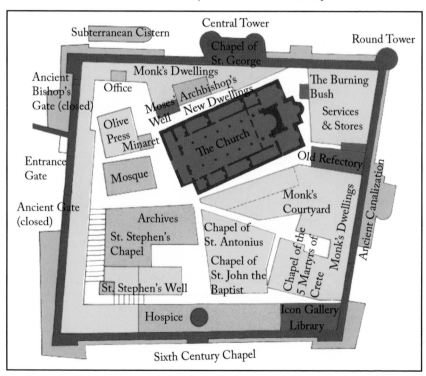

Ground plan of Saint Catherine's Monastery

cannot, and must not, be judged by the criteria of another.

The worst error of all amongst the ill-informed majority in the West is to equate modern civilization with Christianity. For many people, Christianity means "humanism", "progress", "democracy",[2] "a free press" (there is no such thing; the facts and opinions served up by the press merely confirm and comfort majority opinion and sentiment), and the notion that "all-men-are-equal" (ridiculously untrue!). One often hears statements like: "Only Christianity, amongst all the religions, has brought us the blessings of modern science and progress." The post-Vatican II pope Benedict XVI (Josef Ratzinger) even claimed the Enlightenment for Christianity! In fact, in no way did modern science derive from the Christian religion; it is both erroneous and slanderous to say so. Modern science has its origins in the ideas of the seventeenth-century "Age of Reason" and in the eighteenth-century "Enlightenment", when the hitherto dominant Aristotelianism gradually gave way to an empirical, experimental, and materialist manner of thinking. Of course modern science did arise and develop within Christendom; but it was already a weakened Christendom in which Christianity had begun to be discredited, slowly at first, and then, with Darwin in the ninetweenth century, at a greatly increased pace.

When people talk glowingly of the wonders of modern science, it may be that they have in mind modern medicine—but there are also modern nuclear weapons and modern industrial despoliation, not to mention the modern breakdown of morality ("freedom" for things that are evil). Apart from this last, these things are beyond human control, and they continue to ravage humanity. To

[2] See my anthology *Invincible Wisdom* (San Rafael, CA: Sophia Perennis, 2008), pp. 72-73.

equate Christianity with these things is blasphemy, but for the unthinking "average Christian", modern Western science and "progress" are proof positive of the superiority of what they take to be Christianity over what they take to be Islam—or any of the other world religions. Such convictions are hardly conducive to a clear understanding of anything. Those concerned may be excused for knowing little or nothing about the non-Christian religions, but their ignorance of Christianity is far from blameless.

An analogous error is to equate Islam, or any other of the ancient religions, with some unhappy African or Asian country in a state of decadence.[3]

Modern civilization has its origins in the Renaissance, that great inrush of secularization, when nominalism vanquished realism, individualism (or humanism) replaced spirituality, "inwardness" yielded to "outwardness", and both sapiential Christian mysticism and Platonic wisdom retreated from the scene. In a word, society lost its sacred character. The fundamental causes of the genesis and nature of modern civilization have been lucidly set forth in a series of works, published in the earlier part of the twentieth century, by René Guénon,[4] who was also a masterly exponent of the metaphysics and symbolisms of all the religions. An even richer and more far-reaching exposition of religion and metaphysics (coupled with

[3] Some of the highpoints of Islamic civilizational greatness are mentioned on p. xv. One might also mention the Seljuk period in Persia and Turkey, and the best centuries of the Ottoman empire.

[4] Among the principal books of René Guénon are: *Crisis of the Modern World*, *The Reign of Quantity and the Signs of the Times*, *Symbols of Sacred Science*, and *Introduction to the Study of the Hindu Doctrines*.

an insightful critique of the modern deviation) came, in the second part of the twentieth century, from Frithjof Schuon.[5] Amongst other things these authors demonstrated that there is a perfect spiritual equivalence between pre-Renaissance (or Medieval) Christianity and the various Oriental religions. In other words, while the civilization of Christendom was still traditional, it was entirely analogous to the traditional civilizations of the Orient. There is no continuity whatsoever between the spirit or mind-set that gave rise to modern civilization and the authentic Christian tradition. When, therefore, in these pages, comparisons are made between Christianity and Islam, or any other of the religions, it is traditional or Medieval Christianity that is envisaged.

This does not mean that there are today no good Christians! It simply means that society has for long lost its Christian structure. Over the centuries, society has been increasingly deprived of a sacred character, ending up with the replacement of Christianity by humanism and godless political correctness.

*

* *

This chapter is entitled "What does the public know about Islam?"—but one might, by analogy and with equal justification, ask: what does the modern secular public know about any intact and integral religion? The answer is: Very little! One example: The Hindu caste system (*brahmins, kshatriyas, vaishyas, shūdras*) often comes in

---

[5] Among the principal books of Frithjof Schuon are: *The Transcendent Unity of Religions, Logic and Transcendence, Esoterism as Principle and as Way, Form and Substance in the Religions,* and *Road to the Heart: Poems.*

for savage and contemptuous denunciation. Yet a fourfold societal gradation is inherent in the human collectivity. It may be described as follows: there are men who are intelligent, just, and sensitive to "the nature of things"; there are men who have initiative, strength of character, and who are natural leaders; there are skillful craftsmen, productive farmers, and honest merchants (all three of them being collectively the backbone of society); and finally there are unskilled laborers, the "hewers of wood and the drawers of water". This fourfold hierarchical or "vertical" gradation is present in all societies. It is the principle of social harmony; every stratum gets its due. This is all the more easily understood if, bypassing one of the most destructive errors of "political correctness", we are aware of the priority of nature over nurture, and of heredity over environment.

CHAPTER 4

A NOTE ON THE DIFFERENT CATEGORIES
IN THE CONTEMPORARY MUSLIM WORLD

Nowadays, usually for unhappy reasons, there are frequent references in the media to Islam, but little distinction is made between the different categories of attitudes and beliefs amongst the various Muslim groupings. It is true that a rough-and-ready distinction is made between what are deemed to be "moderate" Muslims and "Islamists", but this is not comprehensive or accurate enough, and leaves out of account several important distinctions.

Members of the public have also to some extent become aware that there is a difference between Sunnīs and Shī'is, but they are generally vague as to what this difference might be. The main difference is that the Sunnīs accept the validity of all four of the "rightly-guided" Caliphs, that is to say, the four leaders of the Islamic community who followed immediately on Mohammed (Abu Bakr, Omar, Othman, and Ali), whereas the Shī'is accept only the fourth Caliph (Ali). This difference has run through Muslim history from the earliest times, rather as the controversy regarding the *Filioque*[1] has run through Christian history, bitterly dividing Orthodox and Catholics, from the early Middle Ages onwards. These two theological disputes, Muslim and Christian, have never ceased to cause painful divergences right down to the present day. *Vide*, respectively, the current hostilities between Sunnīs and Shī'is in Iraq and the recent brutal war between Orthodox and Catholics in ex-Yugoslavia.[2]

A considerable confusion arises when the term "fundamentalist" is applied to terrorists and terrorist governments. The term in itself simply means someone who sticks to principles or "fundaments". The terrorists, however, have broken just about every principle of Islam.

The Wahhabis of Saudi Arabia, for their part, are conspicuous by their extreme narrowness and literalism, but they could conceivably be called "fundamentalists", in spite of these constrictive and gravely deforming attitudes. What it is essential to know regarding Wahhabis is that they are very far from representing the full and untruncated religion of Islam.

---

[1] This Latin term (meaning "and from the Son") refers to the theological doctrine that the Holy Spirit proceeds from the Father *and from the Son*. This doctrine was promoted by Western Christians from the sixth century onwards (allegedly to combat the heresy of Arianism), and was officially adopted by the Roman Catholic Church in 1014 A.D. It is rejected by the Eastern Orthodox Church, which retains the formulation of the original Creeds, namely, that the Holy Spirit proceeds "from the Father alone". The official adoption of the *Filioque* by the Roman Church was the cause of "the Great Schism" of 1054 A.D. between the Eastern and the Western Churches.

[2] The Muslims in former Yugoslavia have only too often been subject to assaults from both sides, especially from the Orthodox. A happier example of Eastern Orthodoxy is portrayed in Illustration IV. See also p. 48.

Another misuse of terms is the application of the epithet "conservative" to hardliners within the various revolutionary movements. It is surely the opponents of the revolutionary movements who should be called "conservatives"! A couple of decades ago, a similar misuse of terms was committed when the opponents of Gorbachov (who was in the process of dismantling the Russian revolution) were called "conservatives" instead of communist hardliners, which is what they were.

It may cause surprise when I say that in the twentieth century there was a goodly number of honorable and efficient Muslim statesmen and rulers. Nowadays we are not used to such a thing! Nor do we have sufficient interest in it to take note of it when it occurs. Alas, these rulers are now largely forgotten and unknown. Who has heard of King Idris of Libya (one of the wisest rulers of the twentieth century), Abu Bakar Tafawa Balewa of Nigeria, Tungku 'Abd ar-Rahmān of Malaysia, Adnan Menderes of Turkey, and 'Abd al-Kalām Azad and Abd al-Ghaffur Khan of India? They were all distinguished, competent, and important leaders in their day, but who remembers their names now? The names of all the "bad" people, on the other hand, are household words!

In considering the Muslim rulers of today, we have to distinguish not simply between Sunnīs and Shī'is, but also between those who are "conservatives" (in the true sense of the word) and those who are "revolutionaries", that is to say, between those who are "normal" and those who are "rogues"—this latter term now being in common use in the realm of international affairs. We can in fact distinguish between four categories of Muslim rulers.

1. "Ordinary", or rather, normal men of goodwill, pragmatists or idealists as the case may be (the two are not mutually exclusive), and free from cant. One might think of the recent kings of Jordan and Morocco,

in addition to the names of the twentieth century leaders mentioned above. This group obviously includes not merely "ordinary" men (though this is already a compliment!), but also men of quality and virtue.

2. Wahhabis: "fundamentalists" in a very narrow sense, but far from representing the full and untruncated Islamic tradition. Examples: the recent kings of Saudi Arabia.

3. "Islamic revolutionaries" (followers of Khomeini in Iran), "Islamic Republicans" (followers of Gadhafi in Libya), demagogues and collectivists all. The main Islamic terrorist groupings come into this category. They lay claim to the name of "Islam", but in fact are lethal to everything that is truly Islamic. Their kiss is the kiss of death. Unfortunately, it is people in this category that the Western public looks on as typical Muslims. This category includes both Sunnī and Shī'i groups who, apart from their shared hostility towards the West, are violently opposed to each other.

4. "Islamic" secularists. These include such people as Hafez Assad of Syria and Saddam Hussein of Iraq who, nevertheless, have not hesitated, when it suited their political purpose, to invoke the name of Islam. (One may recall the analogous phenomenon of Stalin re-opening the churches during the nazi onslaught against communist Russia.) Since these people are basically anti-religious, the term "Islamic fundamentalist", in the literal sense, is particularly inappropriate in their case.[3]

---

[3] Although they lived many decades earlier, Mustafa Kemal

A Note on the Different Categories in the Muslim World

Given that the term "fundamentalist" simply means one who sticks to principles or "fundaments", the inaccurate use of this term gives rise to much confusion. The fact that adherents of all of the last three categories—though in fact they differ significantly from one another—are now called "fundamentalists" by the media, causes the blurring of some very real differences, and this must be clearly understood if one wishes to understand contemporary Islamic politics accurately.

It must be admitted that the battle to retain the literal meaning of "fundamentalist" and "fundamentalism" has already been lost. Consequently, when we encounter these terms in the media, it is now up to us to figure out which category is really at stake at any given time.

of Turkey (called "Atatürk" by his admirers) and Gamal 'Abd an-Nasser of Egypt can also be assimilated into category 4. Mustafa Kemal was notorious for his insensate closure of the Turkish *tekkes* (Sufi meeting places), the abolition of the use of the Arabic script for the Turkish language, and the prohibition of Islamic clothing; in short, for his cruel imposition of a secularist state. It is a tragic and fatal irony that it is precisely "Atatürk" (and the Turkey of Atatürk, not of the *tekkes*) that is looked on with favor by an uncomprehending West.

CHAPTER 5

ISLAM IN EUROPE

Nature reveals herself to man through natural laws. Thus, expressing natural law, the Hindus say that it is the *dharma* of birds to fly and of fish to swim. Yet nature, being inexhaustible, cannot be reduced to a system of laws. Transcending any system is nature's "law of exception", which both breaks and "proves" natural laws, since "the exception proves the rule". Thus, in fact, there are fish that fly and birds that swim. Without this "law of exception", or "manifestation of the contrary", natural laws would be absolutist straitjackets, on a plane where the absolute has no place. The possibilities of nature would thereby be limited, *quod absit.*

Europe is Christian, and the Near East is Muslim. Yet there are Christian communities in Palestine, Jordan, Egypt, Lebanon, Syria, Iraq, and Iran;[1] and in Europe there

---

[1] One of the most tragic results of the presence of the Islamic terrorists and similarly minded "Islamist" groups in these countries has been the stirring up of enmity between the Muslim and Christian communities. In recent years this has led to a massive

are the majority Muslim countries of Bosnia, Kosovo, and Albania, and the minority Muslim communities in Macedonia, Bulgaria, and Cyprus.

This reciprocal state of exception is a precious reality, and merely to be aware of it is half-way towards understanding it—and loving it. Only on the basis of the cosmological principle of *Yin-Yang* can one fully comprehend and appreciate its beauty and significance.[2]

*

* *

An interesting phenomenon is Saint Catherine's Monastery, located at the foot of Mount Sinai in Egypt, where Moses received the Ten Commandments. It must be the only monastery in the world which contains within its walls a Muslim mosque and minaret. The monastery is much frequented by the surrounding nomadic Bedouin, who perform numerous services for the monks. See Illustrations IV, top and bottom.

---

emigration of Christians, leaving these ancient Christian communities grievously depleted.

[2] This chapter draws attention to a meaningful historical phenomenon. It does not deal with the entirely different phenomenon of the massive economic migration, since the end of World War II, of Muslims (and members of other religions) from the Indian sub-continent to Britain, of Algerians to France, of Turks to Germany, and of Indonesians to the Netherlands. This phenomenon has been called "the backlash of imperialism".

CHAPTER 6

"THE CLASH OF CIVILIZATIONS"

In recent years, the most notorious form of evil has been "Islamic" terrorism. This has given rise to a widespread acceptance of the misleading phrase "clash of civilizations", first used by Samuel Huntington in his book of the same name. Certainly, the terrorists come from Islamic countries, but they have broken injunction after injunction of the Koran and of Mohammed. Their main achievement is to have created the "Islamophobia" that is today so prevalent in the West; they are beyond doubt the worst enemies that Islam has ever had.

In reality, however, it is not a question of a "clash of civilizations", but of a clash between modern urban terrorism (wrongly called "Islamic") and modern Western humanism (wrongly called "Christian"). It is of paramount importance to understand that there is today no necessary clash between traditional Islam and traditional Christianity. Indeed, in a world that is increasingly unprincipled[1] and

---

[1] Or rather, increasingly attached to the pseudo-principles of "political correctness".

forgetful of God, the two ancient religions are actually on the same side.

What is most offensive to God—judging by the Scriptural texts—and what most upsets the majority of people of goodwill today, is the hatred between the various religious divisions of mankind. The divisions are natural; the hatred is not.[2]

---

[2] See the two Koranic verses 49:13 and 5:48, which are given in full on p. 31.

CHAPTER 7

ISLAM AND THE OTHER RELIGIONS

Many Muslims find it hard to come to terms with non-Islamic religions for entirely understandable reasons. Firstly, as the last of the religions, Islam incorporates within itself all antecedent Semitic prophets (from Adam up to Mary and Jesus), and indeed claims to return to the primordial monotheism of the "proto-Semite" Abraham. Being very aware of this, Muslims tend to think that not only does Islam "confirm" all previous revelations, but that it also "supersedes" them.

Secondly, the Christian doctrines of the Trinity and the Incarnation are fundamentally alien to both Muslim and Jewish thinking, appearing to Semitic sensibility, to impugn Divine Unity and to blasphemously "associate" a creature with the transcendent God. Likewise, the Aryan religions of Hinduism and Buddhism (and ancient Greece and Rome) appear to Muslims, not only as "incarnationist" like Christianity, but also as polytheistic and idolatrous.

In point of fact, most Muslims, just like the adherents of every religion, know very little about religions other than their own. Almost invariably, what most "religionists" think they know about the other religions is incomplete, superficial, distorted, and biased. Inevitably, they can see every religion other than their own only "from the outside". They abusively (and fatally) judge foreign religions by the criteria of their own. Furthermore, and especially since the destruction of the twin towers by "Islamic" terrorists in New York in 2001, flagrant "double standards" dominate the scene and virtually obliterate any trace of objectivity. But the fact that "religionists" are inadequately and inaccurately informed, does not prevent their superficial, patchy, and inaccurate knowledge from governing their thinking, sentiments, speech, and actions—and, as a result, having highly undesirable practical consequences. Scanty knowledge, superficiality, and frank error become unquestioned and unexamined convictions, and raw assertions take the place of facts and arguments.

Nevertheless, contrary to general belief, there exist in Islam a goodly number of weighty precedents that open the way to a wide, deep, and subtle grasp of the "other religions".

Jalāl ad-Dīn Rūmī (1207-1273), for example, not only accepted Christian disciples, but even had an understanding of "fire-worshipers" (Zoroastrians).

The great jurist and philosopher, Al-Ghazālī (1058-1111), was aware that, contrary to the general Muslim belief, the Christian Gospels had not been "altered" (at least not in a *literal* sense)[1] and, in spite of the general

---

[1] In this connection it is necessary to understand that it is false to say that all religions are "the same", as "New-Agers" allege. The reason for being of religious plurality is precisely that, in their outward forms, all religions are different. Firstly, the one *essence* cannot but have many *forms*. Secondly, God speaks in a variety of "languages" (in order to accommodate the needs of the different racial, ethnic, and cultural sectors of humanity),

Islamic suspicion of "incarnationism", he had—like the Algerian Sheikh Ahmad al-Alawi (1869-1934)—a certain notion of the metaphysical meaning of the Christian doctrine of the Trinity.[2] As regards Hinduism, I have elsewhere alluded to the fact that Dara Shikoh, son of the Emperor Shah Jahan and the Empress Mumtaz Mahal, declared: "The science of Vedanta and the science of Sufism are one." Dara Shikoh also had the *Bhagavad Gītā*, the *Yoga Vasīshtha*, and several of the *Upanishads* translated into Persian.

Most explicit of all are the oft-quoted words of Ibn 'Arabī:

My heart has become capable of every form: it is a pasture for gazelles, a cloister for Christian monks, a temple for idols, the Kaaba of the pilgrim, the tablets of the Torah, and the Book of the Koran. I practice the religion of Love. In whatsoever directions its caravans advance, the religion of Love shall be my religion and my faith.

La-qad sār qalbī qālbilān kullu suwaratin: famar'as li-ghaslān, wa dīn li-ruhbāni, wa baitun li-authānin, wa ka'batu tāhyaghin, wa 'l-wāhu

and He does not speak the same "language" twice. (This does not mean that God does not permit legitimate and providential "divisions" in the religions, such as Hīnayāna and Mahāyāna Buddhism, Shivaite and Vishnuite Hinduism, Roman Catholic and Eastern Orthodox Christianity, and Sunni and Shī'i Islam.)

[2] *Ar-radd al-jamīl li-ilāhiyat 'Īsā bi-sarīh al-Injīl* (MS. AS 2246[1] *waqf* of Sultan Mahmūd II, Istanbul, translated and discussed by Louis Massignon in *La Revue des Études Islamiques*, 1932, section IV).

*tūrātin, wa mus-hafu qur'āni. A dīnu b-dīni 'l-
habbi. Annī tawajjahat rakāyibu-hu, fa 'd-dīnu
dīnī wa īmānī.*

Tarjumān al-Ashwāq
("The Interpreter of Love"), XI, 13-15

The final authority is the Koran itself:

We [God] have inspired Messengers of whom
We have already told thee [O Mohammed,] and
Messengers *of whom We have not told thee.*

Sūra "Women", 4:164

Verily We have raised in every nation a Messenger,
proclaiming: Serve God and shun false gods.

Sūra "The Bee", 16:36

We [God] make no distinction between any of
them [the Messengers].

Sūra "The Cow", 2:136

We caused Jesus, son of Mary, to follow them
[the Hebrew prophets], and gave him the Gospel,
and placed compassion and mercy in the hearts of
those who follow him.

Sūra "Iron", 57:27

*
* *

Let us end these quotations with a sweet message from
Rumi:

If you want Heaven, become the companion of
Jesus!

Islam and the Other Religions

*
* *

As regards the three Semitic or Abrahamic monotheisms, one can perhaps characterize them as follows: Judaism is a "Law", Christianity is a "Spirit", and Islam is a "Law" and a "Spirit". Islam is like Judaism as regards "Law", and like Christianity as regards "Spirit". "Spirit" is greater than "Law", and therefore Islam is more like Christianity than like Judaism. The "Spirit" in Islam coincides with Sufism.

This characterization, expressed in a slightly different way, also reveals an important difference between Christianity and Islam: Christianity is "Love" and Islam is "Knowledge" ("gnosis" or, in Hindu terms, *jñāna*). This "Knowledge" *contains* "Love", just as "Love" is inextricably wed with "Knowledge".[3]

---

[3] Christianity by no means excludes "Knowledge" or "Gnosis": "Ye shall know the Truth, and the Truth shall make you free" (John 8:32). Likewise, Judaism by no means excludes "Knowledge" and "Love". There are the Wisdom of Solomon ("Knowledge") and the Psalms of David ("Love").

CHAPTER 8

RELIGIOUS AND ETHNIC CONFLICT
IN THE LIGHT OF THE WRITINGS OF
THE TRADITIONALIST OR
PERENNIALIST SCHOOL

If one wished to sum up in one word the central evil of the modern age, one could do so with the word "atheism". While this diagnosis might command ready agreement on the part of religiously-minded people, it might still, because it seems too abstract or too general, be regarded as a trifle facile. Nevertheless, I believe that, in one or more of its many guises, it is precisely atheism that is at the root of all modern evils. Atheism may be as ancient as fallen man, but the atheism that is with us today has its direct origin in the ideas of the eighteenth century "enlightenment"—the ideas espoused by Voltaire, Rousseau, and the *encylopédistes*.

Of course, I use the term "atheism" in an extremely comprehensive way, and I include in it things not usually perceived as being directly atheistic, such as illogic, unimaginativeness, indifference, and complacency—all so many denials of God (and thus so many abdications of humanity) without which such absurd but successful hoaxes as evolutionism, psychologism, and Marxism would never have been possible.

In the twentieth century, the most explicit and brutal form of atheism was Soviet communism.[1] In 1989, after more than seventy years of pretense and pretension during which it enjoyed the enthusiastic approval of "enlightened" academia—it foundered utterly. Needless to say, the evil and the ignorance that took concrete form in communism have not simply evaporated. Alas, they have simply found other forms.

When something is perceived as bad, there are usually reactions to it, and these in turn can be either good or bad. There was the reaction to worldliness by Saint Francis of Assisi, a "second Christ" (*alter Christus*) who, through the strength of his faith and his asceticism, reanimated and reinvigorated the Christian tradition for centuries to come. One could perhaps think of other renewals of this kind, but such reactions to the bad are rare indeed. Nowadays, most reactions to what is perceived as evil are themselves evil: they are reactions, not *par en haut* ("in an upward direction"), but *par en bas* ("in a downward direction"). It is as if the devil took charge of the reactions against his own work—and used them to his further advantage.

Examples of bad reactions to atheism or secularism are not hard to find. In keeping with the age we live in, they are invariably forms of collectivism of one sort or another. Collectivism means the generation of quantitative power from below. Its opposite is spontaneous submission to qualitative power from above. This latter involves individual responsibility and the ability to recognize legitimate authority. In the past, people *submitted* to the

---

[1] And also, of course, the long period of communism in China.

self-evident truths of religion; today many people espouse, in mass movements, the *outward trappings* of religion. Khomeiniism and Gadhafiism are cases in point. So are the majority of other contemporary nationalisms. This form of collectivism usually takes the form of aggressive "denominationalism".

Like other collectivisms, denominationalism is anything but eirenic; it is the direct source of a viciously aggressive competitiveness between religious and cultural communities, which is properly known as "communalism"—a term that was first used in this sense in India. Communalism, in the form of inter-religious conflict, has today become a worldwide epidemic. But do we know its exact nature? It is the rivalry, to the death, of two neighboring *religious* nationalisms. We have been witnesses to the war between Azerbaijanis and Armenians and to the war between Roman Catholic Croats and Eastern Orthodox Serbs. Both of these rival nationalisms are deeply disturbing. Particularly odious is the case of the Serbians, who conducted a cruel and destructive onslaught on Slavic Muslim Bosnia (particularly the historic cities of Sarajevo and Mostar), and on Albanian Muslim Kosovo. In Sri Lanka the communal rivalry is between Buddhists and Hindus, in the Punjab between Hindus and Sikhs, in Ayodhyā and elsewhere in India it is between Muslims and Hindus, in Cyprus between Greeks and Turks, and in Northern Ireland between Catholics and Protestants. Each grouping adheres to its denomination and its culture in a passionate but nevertheless superficial and formalistic way, and in a manner which lethally challenges a neighboring and (usually) equally superficial and formalistic cultural loyalty. These groupings are often called fundamentalist, but in their ideology they are invariably modern, progressivist, and collectivist. Communalism has been well described as "collective egoism". The last thing that one expects to find in these fanatical groupings is spirituality or piety. Not the Inward, but the outward in its most brutal and superficial mode, is their concern. They defend the form while killing the essence; they will kill for the husk, while trampling on the life-giving kernel. They kill not only their putative religious rival: they have already killed themselves. Communalism, like all shallow—but consuming—passion, is suicidal.

It might be said that one can find a prefiguration of communalism in the "holy wars" of ages past—the Crusades, for example—in which two traditional systems were pitted against one another, one viewing the other as the representative of evil. It is a far cry, however, from the wars of the Middle Ages to the mindless hatreds and mechanized exterminations of modern times.

There is no doubt, however, that the seismic "crack" or "fault" which runs through former Yugoslavia, Ukraine, and elsewhere in Eastern Europe does have its origin in an ancient division, namely, the "Great Schism" of 1054 A.D. It is the dividing line between Eastern and Western Christendom. I doubt if there is any more bitterly-manned frontier in the whole world. This is a chilling reminder in the contemporary Western climate of facile and superficial ecumenism.

In view of the ancient origin of most of the present-day communal divisions, it could perhaps be objected that communalism is no more than the instinct of self-preservation, and that, as such, it is as old as mankind. However, this is far from being the case. For very many centuries, the world was divided into great empires, each comprising a variety of peoples and often a variety of religions. The Anglo-Greek traveler and author Marco Pallis once made mention of an eighteenth century Tibetan book which (from the standpoint of Tibet) referred to the four great empires, which to them seemed to encompass the world: the Chinese, the Mughal, the Russian, and the Roman. By this last term they meant Christendom or Europe.

It was at the end of World War I that several empires that had encompassed many different peoples and religions crumbled: the Prussian, the Austro-Hungarian, the Ottoman. Many new countries appeared: Poland, Czechoslovakia, Yugoslavia, amongst others. Also some independent Arab countries emerged from the Ottoman Turkish empire. All this required an "ideological" basis, and this was found in 1918 in the "Fourteen Points" of President Woodrow Wilson, one of which was "self-determination", the first time these fateful words achieved prominence. The idea may have been well-intentioned—a safeguard against putative imperial oppression—but it has since become a dogma of the modern world and of the United Nations, and is the "philosophical" justification of almost all current communalism and ethnic conflict.

To paraphrase the words of the late Professor John Lodge, often quoted by Ananda Coomaraswamy: from the four great empires known to the Tibetans (Chinese, Mughal, Russian, and "Roman" [i.e. European]) to the present-day "United Nations", *quelle dégringolade!*

*
* *

Let us leave communalism for a moment, and turn to a very different phenomenon of our times. This is what the American Academy of Religion has called "the perennialist or esoterist school", also known as "the traditionalist school", of which the founders were the French philosopher and orientalist René Guénon (1886-1951) and the German philosopher, poet, and artist Frithjof Schuon (1907-1998), and which was further expounded by Ananda Coomaraswamy (1877-1947) and Titus Burckhardt (1908-1984).[2] The principal characteristics of this school include the fundamental and essential principles of metaphysics (with its cosmological and anthropological ramifications), intellectual intuition, orthodoxy, tradition, universality, the science of symbolism; spirituality in the broadest sense; intrinsic morals and esthetics; and the meaning and importance of sacred art. A very important characteristic is a deep-reaching critique of the modern world, on the basis of strictly traditional principles. Above all, like Pythagoras and Plato, Guénon and Schuon derive their doctrinal expositions directly from *intellectus purus*—a process which lends to these expositions an unsurpassable lucidity, not to say infallibility.

This supra-formal truth constitutes the *religio perennis*. This term, which does not imply a rejection of the similar terms *philosophia perennis* and *sophia perennis*, nevertheless contains a hint of an additional dimension which is unfailingly present in Schuon's writings. This is that intellectual understanding entails a spiritual responsibility, that intelligence requires to be complemented by sincerity and faith, and that "seeing" (in height) implies "believing" (in depth). In other words, the greater our perception of essential and saving truth, the greater our obligation towards an effort of inward of spiritual "realization".

I have called this perennialist current of intellectuality and spirituality "a phenomenon of our times"—but unlike other phenomena of today, it is, by its very nature, a "secret" one, a "still small voice", a hidden presence, sought out and found only by those with a hunger and

---

[2] For a detailed description of the perennialist school, see my book *Remembering in a World of Forgetting* (Bloomington, IN: World Wisdom, 2008), chapter entitled "Frithjof Schuon and the Perennialist School".

thirst for it, and known only to those with eyes to see and ears to hear.

*

* *

Returning to communalism: at the outward level, this is sometimes addressed in a desultory and piecemeal way by what is called "the international community". And, in this connection, the United States has become embroiled in several wars. Inevitably, the response to such efforts is highly uneven, and experience has shown that there is no one who can effectively—and impartially—"police" the entire world. Such sympathy as is extended to victims is on a humanitarian basis towards *individuals;* the public mind does not comprehend or consider the worth or value of *collectivities,* specifically ethnic or religious collectivities, which are still wholly or partially "traditional". And yet it is religious communities—such as, for example Tibetan Buddhists and Bosnian Muslims, that are in the greatest danger of being destroyed by a powerful ideological or denominationalist neighbor—something much less likely to happen when they were part of a large, but tolerant (because "realistic") empire. Bosnia, for example, was part of the Austro-Hungarian empire. This empire encompassed, ethnically speaking, Germans, Magyars, and Slavs and, religiously speaking, Roman Catholicism, Eastern Orthodoxy, and Islam. I have myself seen in the principal mosque in Sarajevo an exquisite Persian prayer carpet of immense dimensions donated by the Emperor Franz Josef. This is a courtesy unlikely to be extended to the Slavic Muslims by the aggressive religious nationalism of their Eastern Orthodox neighbors, whose sentiments, on the contrary, have shown themselves to be fiercely destructive and even exterminatory. Both Frithjof Schuon and Titus Burckhardt have mentioned in their writings that kings and nobles often had a wisdom and a tolerance unknown in a denominationally-motivated clergy, who unfortunately have it in their power to influence the people along passional, denominational, and ideological, lines. A similar point was made by Dante, who, for intellectual and spiritual reasons, sided with the Emperor, and not the Pope.

*

* *

Communalism derives from denominationalism. Communalism is obviously outward; denominationalism, being an attitude of mind, could perhaps be described as "falsely inward". There is virtually nothing that we as individuals can do outwardly about communalism; but we can always keep under review our attitudes towards our own denomination, and be on guard against any slipping into what I have called "denominationalism" (which the French call *confessionalisme*). We must not, even within ourselves, give comfort to communalism by consciously or unconsciously participating in the denominationalism that makes it possible.

As I have mentioned, the traditionalist writings are largely an exposition of the *religio perennis*, the "underlying religion" of essential truth and saving grace which is at the heart of each great revelation (and of which each great revelation is the providential "clothing" for a particular sector of humanity). Because of this relationship between the "underlying religion" and its various "providential clothings", it is necessary for anyone wishing access to this "underlying religion" to do so by espousing one particular traditional and orthodox religion, to believe and understand its central theses (its "dogmas"), and to participate in its way of sanctification (its "sacraments"). The universalism of the perennialist does not mean dispensing with sacred forms that were revealed by God for our salvation. There is no other way than through these. The perennialist is simply aware that the Formless must needs be represented on earth by a plurality of forms. The contrary is metaphysically impossible.

To return to the *philosophia perennis* or *religio perennis*: one finds two types of people attracted to it. There are those who are already say, Catholics or Muslims, and who find that the insights of the *religio perennis* produce a deepening and an essentialization of their pre-existing faith; and there are those—possibly products of the post-religious modern world—who have discovered and been conquered by the *religio perennis*, and who as a result embrace, say, Catholicism, Eastern Orthodoxy, or Islam in order sincerely to live, actualize, or realize, the truth or the truths that they have discovered. The first group are Catholics or Muslims first and *religio perennis* second; the second group are *religio perennis* first and Catholics or Muslims second.

Those in the first category already possessed something of value, something sacred; as a result, they may hesitate to embrace fully all the theses of the *religio perennis*. Those in the second category, on the other hand, owe everything to the *religio perennis*; absolutely nothing else could have awakened them to the sacred and distanced them from the illusions of the modern world; as a result, they may hesitate to embrace fully all the secondary demands of the denomination they have adopted, especially those of a communal or partisan nature.

These two positions are to some extent extremes; there are many positions that lie between them. Also, the two positions are not necessarily unchanging. Sometimes a person, who has come to Christianity through the *religio perennis*, slips into the life of his denomination, and "metaphysics", "universalism", etc., cease to be in the forefront of his spiritual life. Sometimes, on the other hand, a person who has been a "denominationalist", suddenly or gradually sees the full meaning of the *religio perennis*, is overwhelmed by its luminosity, crystallinity, and celestiality, and henceforth his sacramental and prayer life is governed, so to speak, by it alone. When all is said and done, however, one has to say that the two approaches do remain distinct, and each has its own characteristics and consequences.

Let me make here some strongly critical remarks regarding the Vatican II Council (1962-65).[3] It is not necessary to be a perennialist in order to condemn the official Roman Church of today; it is sufficient simply to know the traditional Catholic catechism. The discrepancy between the two is striking. The perennialist sympathizes with the most exoteric of Roman Catholics, provided he be orthodox. But he himself is not a Roman Catholic exoterist. The Catholic exoterist dreams of the "Catholicism of the 1930s", he gives his allegiance to a denomination, to a form. In so doing, he has much justification, for Catholicism in its historic, outward form endured to beyond the middle of the twentieth century. There have been many important and remarkable saints in recent times: in the nineteenth century, Saint Theresa of Lisieux, Saint Jean-Baptiste Vianney (the Curé d'Ars), Saint Bernadette of Lourdes and, in the twentieth century, Saint Maria Goretti.

Nevertheless, in spite of this unbroken tradition of dogma, sacrament, and sanctity, it is important to be aware that the Catholic Church of the 1930s had long since incorporated within itself many fatal flaws, all deriving ultimately from its suicidal espousal of the vainglory of

---

[3] See also p. 2.

the Renaissance. The irruption of Protestantism is usually seen as a reaction against the sale of indulgences and other abuses, but it could also be said that Luther, who loved Saint Paul and Saint Augustine, was in his fashion a man of the Middle Ages who rebelled against the treason and "humanism" of the Renaissance. The Reformation did not kill Catholicism; in fact it provoked the Council of Trent at which the Catholic Church went as far as it could towards putting its house in order, thus enabling it to maintain its witness for several more centuries. The death blow to the official Catholic Church was delivered only in the twentieth century by Teilhard de Chardin and "Vatican II".

Such strong criticism of the present-day Catholic Church may come as a surprise to readers; but the situation was foreseen by the last traditional Pope, Pius XII, when he said that the day was coming soon when the faithful would only be able to celebrate the holy sacrifice of the Mass on the secret altar of the heart. Many thought that he was referring to the threat of outward persecution, but, with hindsight, one can see that his words applied only too well to the impending arrival of a falsified church and a falsified liturgy. Be that as it may, the perennialist or esoterist owes allegiance, not to a form as such, but only to the Holy Spirit, only to the supra-formal Truth. He knows the meaning of forms; he respectfully and humbly participates in sacred forms revealed to vehicle his salvation; but he knows that forms are but messengers of the Formless, and that the Formless or Supra-formal, of necessity, possesses on earth more that one system of forms. The extrinsic reason for this plurality is the great ethnic and psychological divisions of mankind. The intrinsic reason is that the Supra-formal is inexhaustible, and each successive revelation, in its outward form, manifests a fresh aspect thereof. In its outward form, I say, because each revelation, in its inward essence, does give access to, and does confer the grace of, the Supra-formal. That is why each one saves. This reality is what Schuon has called the supra-formal, or transcendent, unity of the religions.

It has been emphasized that universalism does not imply the rejection of forms. Does it imply syncretism? The answer is "No". The doctrine of the transcendent or esoteric unity of the religions represents not a syncretism, but synthesis. What does this mean? It means that we must *believe* in all orthodox, traditional religions, but we can *practice* only one. Consider the metaphor of climbing a mountain. Climbers can start from different positions at the foot of the mountain. From these positions, they must follow the particular path that will lead them to the top. We can and must believe in the efficacy of all the paths, but our legs are not long enough to enable us to put our feet on two paths at once! Nevertheless, the other paths can sometimes be of help to us. For example, if we notice that someone on a neighboring path has a particularly skillful way of circumventing a boulder, it may be that we can use the same skill to negotiate such boulders as may lie ahead of us on our own path. The paths as such, however, meet only at the summit. The religions are one only in God.

Perhaps I could say in passing that, while it is a grave matter to change one's religion, the mountain-climbing metaphor nevertheless illustrates what takes place when one does. One moves horizontally across the mountain and joins an alternative path, and at that point one starts climbing again. One does not have to go back to the foot of the mountain and start again from there.

*
* *

In this chapter, I have moved back and forward between the *religio perennis* and the current worldwide epidemic of ethnic and religious strife known as communalism. I have done so because both are significant phenomena of our time. The one is only too outward; the other is inward and in a sense hidden. As regards the apparently intractable communal rivalries, there is little outwardly that we as individuals can do. Inwardly, however, we can help in two ways, firstly by our prayers, and secondly—and as a function of our prayer—by deepening our understanding of the relationship between forms and the Formless, and of the relationship which, ideally, should exist between the several forms themselves. Each revealed belief system (with its corresponding way of worship) is a particular manifestation of the *religio perennis*. It is therefore no mistake to regard any one revelation as *the* revelation, as long as one is not "nationalistic" or "competitive" about it. In practice, however, it can be a difficult matter. How can one, at one moment, enjoin people to be committed "traditional" Christians, and then, the next moment, speak with equal respect of the religions of Krishna, Buddha, or Mohammed? Difficult indeed. But, in some way, it has to be done.

The basic cultural distinction made by the post-Christian world is still between Christendom and all the rest, but this is simply not a sufficient analysis for the present age. The distinction that we have to make today is between believers and non-believers, between the "good" and the "bad"—irrespective of their revealed form. In so doing we need not be afraid of being called "judgemental"! That secular humanists should make this reproach is the height of hypocrisy, for they are the worst offenders. Nothing escapes their critical attention, but, lacking in depth, their conclusions are inevitably false. They slowly but surely lead to the destruction of age-old norms.

"Judge not that ye be not judged" (Matt. 7:1). As I already mentioned, this is a text that is too easily misinterpreted. It applies to our egoism, our subjectivism, our self-interest; it does not preclude the reality of objectivity, still less does it abolish the truth. There is manifestly plenty for us to "judge" and, having judged, to oppose: atheism, agnosticism, political correctness, feminism, etc., and all the false ideas that flow from the "Enlightenment" and the French Revolution. We passively tolerate so much that comes from Satan ("rock" music, fashionable "-isms", sacrilegious entertainments, blasphemous art) and yet we think our culture is threatened if someone wears a form of dress or speaks a language different from our own. We must be sufficiently alert to discriminate between what comes from God (no matter how exotic its outward form) and what does not (no matter how familiar).

Our judgements must be totally divorced from denomination. We must be able to oppose the "bad" (even though they be of our own religion), and acclaim the "good" (even though they belong to a strange religion). This injunction may sound platitudinous, but almost no one follows it instinctively. We must be capable of the cardinally important intuition that *every religion*—be it Christianity, Hinduism, Buddhism, or Islam—*comes from God and every religion leads back to God;* in these latter days, we ignore and underestimate the "other religions" at our peril. Alas, very few (be they Christians, Muslims, Hindus, Buddhists, or other) are able to make this angelic leap of faith—for many bad reasons, as well as for one good reason, namely that each religion has within it a verse corresponding to "No man cometh to the Father but by Me" (John 14:6).

It is precisely this "absolute" in each religion that makes it a religion, but it is difficult for most people to realize the *simple* truth that the absolute, being by definition supra-formal, must needs—within the formal world—espouse many forms. It cannot be otherwise, despite the providentially "absolutist" text within each religion. To understand this truth, at least theoretically, is the *first* necessity in the present age. But unfortunately, like so many good things, this area has been partially taken over by the devil, in the shape of the cults, the "New Age" movement, etc. One might say that it is in this area above all that the teachings and elucidations of the perennialists have an indispensable role to play.

CHAPTER 9

THE GULF BETWEEN TRADITIONAL
AND NATURALISTIC ART

This book is about Islam, but the other traditional and orthodox religions are never completely absent from it. Amongst other things, this enables one to see the various analogies and similarities that exist between the different religions.

In the spiritualities or mysticisms of all the religions—including Islamic mysticism or Sufism—the element "beauty" plays a significant role. In the Foreword to the present book, Dr. Oldmeadow writes: "One of the most telling symptoms of the dark confusion within parts of the Islamic world is the overt hostility to Sufism". In practice this means, amongst other things, that beauty has practically vanished from the religious scene—despite Mohammed's well-known *hadīth* (saying): "God is beautiful and He loves beauty." It must be said at once, however, that today this element is no longer fully appreciated or exploited in any of the world religions.

The role of beauty does not only involve "beauty of behavior" or "beauty of character", which is obviously of first importance in the leading of a spiritual life; it also involves "beauty of forms"—in every imaginable outward context, from the Cathedral of Chartres and the Temple of Angkor Wat down to vestimentary art, domestic decor, and the most modest of everyday utensils. All this is the domain of art, and this domain is all-encompassing.

These remarks in no way refer to the type of "beauty" that we are encouraged to appreciate by familiarizing ourselves in art galleries with Renaissance and Baroque art. In Western Christendom, as is explained below, it means pre-Renaissance or Medieval art (that is to say, "traditional" art).

Every authentic religion brings with it, and lives within, a climate of beauty. One may immediately think of some well-known highlights: Hindu temples and Hindu saris, Buddhist sculpture and Japanese kimonos, Islamic architecture and calligraphy, Byzantine and Russian churches and icons, Romanesque churches and Gospel manuscripts, Gothic architecture and sculpture. Quite apart from these artistic peaks, one must also consider the general ambience in which "ordinary people" lived: their dress, their abodes, their social mores, their arts and crafts, their traditional piety—in other words, the overall beauty and harmony of their life in a traditional society.[1]

The first objection that one might make to this litany of praise is: what about their poverty, what about their suffering? Well, the latter must be compared with the suffering of modern times. There were the nazi concentration camps and the gulag archipelago, and there are the "secret prisons" of today; there was the carnage of World War I and of the war in Vietnam; there was

---

[1] Ananda Coomaraswamy was fond of saying that modern civilization is the only one that is characterized by its ugliness.

the atrocity of the nuclear bombing of Hiroshima and Nagasaki in World War II, and later the disasters of the nuclear accidents at Chernobyl and Fukushima; not only did these cause countless deaths, but also dreadful genetic after-effects in survivors. Suffering is always with us, but it takes different forms—some manifestly worse than others. As regards the poverty of the traditional peoples, the Swiss cultural anthropologist Titus Burckhardt remarked that they are "outwardly poor, but inwardly rich". This certainly cannot be said of modern man! Modern man may or may not be outwardly rich but, inwardly, he is impoverished; he has no certainties, he lives in a tissue of relativities; he has no inward peace, he has no defense against that curious amalgam of *Angst* and optimism that is now widespread. As regards the "richness" of modern times, the English author Lord Northbourne commented: "We now live in an age of plenty, but what use is plenty of rubbish?" Are we really richer because everyone has a cell phone?

In Western Christendom, truly traditional civilization ceased to exist many centuries ago. The sea-change (or "the great divide", to use C. S. Lewis' term) came towards the end of the thirteenth and beginning of the fourteenth century. The break became even more explicit two hundred years later with the humanistic revolution that was the Renaissance. The final and most devastating assault was delivered by the overtly anti-religious eighteenth century Enlightenment; and that is leaving unmentioned the degeneration of recent times.

The first distinction to be made in the field of art is whether it is "traditional" or "non-traditional" (that is to say, "naturalistic").

Then, within traditional art itself, there is a

distinction to be made between what is "sacred" and what is "profane": "sacred art" refers to the creation of places of worship, liturgical objects, icons, manuscripts of the Scriptures, etc.; "profane art" includes such things as pottery, metal work, woodwork, masonry, etc. It is important to understand that, in this context, profane art was and is just as "traditional" as sacred art.[2]

In "non-traditional", "naturalistic", or post-Medieval art, the "sacred" element has completely vanished, and all art is on the same, non-transcendent, non-sacramental level. There is no longer "sacred" art; there is only "religious" art in a naturalistic style.[3]

*

* *

Naturalism violates the nature of things because, in painting, it treats the plane surface as if it were three-dimensional space, and the immobility of the surface as if it could contain movement; and in sculpture, naturalism treats inert matter as if it were living flesh, and then as if it were engaged in motion.

Frithjof Schuon

---

[2] The term "profane" may sound derogatory, but its fundamental meaning is simply "outside the temple". It is not a value-judgement: it is neutral. Here it means "non-liturgical". For example: a plow is not "sacred" (i.e., liturgical), it is "profane" (i.e., extra-liturgical), but a plow is entirely honorable and traditional. The contemporary use of the word "profanity" to mean vulgarity is a deviation from the original meaning.

[3] See Titus Burckhardt, *Sacred Art in East and West* (Bloomington, IN: World Wisdom, 2001).

"Violating the nature of things": in painting, this refers to the fact that naturalistic painting demands from paper something which its planimetric nature cannot give. To force an apparently three-dimensional depth onto paper, parchment, or wood by means of perspective "violates the nature" of painting.

In this connection, Ananda Coomaraswamy often quotes the words of Saint Thomas Aquinas: "Art is the imitation of nature *in her mode of operation.*" The operative words are those in italics. In obedience to this axiom, the traditional artist does not punctiliously copy the surface of nature; on the contrary, he re-enacts (like a priest) the mystery of Divine creation by introducing into human creativity the Aristotelian concepts of *eidos* ("essence", which is masculine and intellectual—and "vertical") and *hyle* ("substance", which is feminine and "material"—and "horizontal"). The symbolism of weaving is particularly eloquent in this regard.[4]

"Violating the nature of things" in sculpture means that naturalistic sculpture demands from stone or metal something which, given their inert nature, they cannot give, namely that they are forced to take on the aspect of a living and moving creature. Inevitably, the result is grotesque. This is visible at its worst in Baroque art. It is an "outward" without an "inward"—the very definition of idolatry!

The insensitive use of these tricks of naturalism is completely absent from traditional art.

Consider also the symbolism of a hammer and chisel working on stone. The carefully directed chisel

---

[4] On the symbolism of weaving, see the important study by Aristide Messinesi, "A Craft as a Fountain of Grace and a Means of Spiritual Realization", *Tomorrow*, 1965, Vol. 13, No. 1.

(intellective-active), and the "spiritual" effort of the hammer (volitive-active) on the stone (inert-passive) are eloquent. In this symbolism, intelligence and will are "vertical" and the material worked on is "horizontal".

*
* *

Perhaps I can turn here to a complaint that women sometimes make, because it helps to illustrate the point at issue. They allege that men admire them only for their bodies, and do not credit them with having a brain! This grievance, whether justified or not, serves as a useful means of indicating the limitations of naturalistic art, for what these women allege is precisely what naturalistic art does. In its representation of the human figure (for example, a female such as the Hellenistic "Venus de Milo" or a male such as the Renaissance "David" by Michelangelo), naturalistic art produces a perfect copy of a perfect human body, while completely by-passing the essential, namely, that the human body is the vehicle, not simply of a brain but, much more importantly, of *an immortal soul*!

This, precisely, is the role of "traditional" statuary. Some say that, in powerfully expressing human immortality, traditional art neglects the exactness of form—but this is not quite accurate. For example, in a Tibetan statue of the Buddha, one sees clearly a perfect male form, but one also sees and "feels" Peace, coupled with Compassion. In a Romanesque statue of Christ in Majesty, one sees clearly a perfect male form, but one also sees and "feels" Inwardness and Salvation, coupled with implacable Judgement. In a Romanesque statue of the Holy Virgin, one sees clearly a perfect female form, but one also sees and "feels" Mercy, coupled with Purity and Primordial Perfection. This is the celestial "mystery" of traditional art. It is a sort of *incarnatio* or *sarcosis;* it is a

78

sacrament, an outward "conveyor" of an inward presence. Aside from these celestial figures, and regarding the human form as such, traditional statuary invariably manifests the essential features of man: intelligence and strength, as well as dignity and stability (especially, but not exclusively, in the male) and beauty and love, as well as innocence and inviolability (especially, but not exclusively, in the female).

The fundamental problem of Western art is that, with the Renaissance—and from then onwards—the ancient science of symbolism was lost. It is this absence that so brutally and abruptly distinguishes Renaissance art and subsequent styles from the art of the Middle Ages and the Orient.

The Renaissance and Baroque styles are very different, but one is tempted to say of both that they are "body without soul". This would not be completely true, however, as each of them, within certain limits, can represent emotions. What one can say with certainty is that both of them are cases of "art without spirit", or "art without 'intellect'", in the Medieval or Eckhartian sense of these terms.

The principles of the sacred science of symbolism were finely enunciated in the writings of Saint Dionysius the Areopagite. (Modern scholarship scorns the conflation of several Saint Denises, and calls the early theologian "pseudo-Dionysius".) Titus Burckhardt quotes his words to good effect in his book *Chartres and the Birth of the Cathedral.*

The basic principle of art is also to be found in the succinct axiom from the "Emerald Tablet" of Hermes Trismegistos (the "thrice-great" Hermes): "That which is below is like unto that which is above, and that which is above is like unto that which is below." This principle is symbolized by the two inverted triangles of the Seal of

Solomon: ✡. This reminds us once again of the "priestly" role of the traditional artist.

I refer above only to statuary, but the same traditional principles apply in all arts: in architecture (for example: Byzantine, Romanesque, and Gothic churches and cathedrals); in painting (for example, Hindu, Buddhist, and Taoist painting, Ethiopian, Coptic, and Mozarabic manuscripts, Eastern Orthodox icons); in calligraphy (for example, Chinese manuscripts, Koranic manuscripts, and Medieval—especially Celtic—manuscripts of the Gospels); in the human voice (for example, Gregorian chant, Russian Church chants, Koranic psalmody, the chanting of Tibetan monks, the singing of the Native Americans); in musical instruments (as used, for example, in India, Japan, Bali, etc.); in pottery (for example, Chinese, Islamic, Navajo); in carpets (for example, Islamic, Tibetan, Chinese, Navajo); in dancing (Hindu, Buddhist, African, and the Sun Dance of the Plains Indians).

An interesting correspondence that occurs in traditional Christian architecture can be seen in the ground-plan of a church, which visibly corresponds to the body of Christ: the high altar is the heart, the apse is the head, the transept is the arms, and the nave and the aisles are the lower body, the legs, and the feet.

What is demanded of us is "deep meditation" on the meaning of sacred symbolism as it has been expressed in traditional lore and art from the earliest times. The Renaissance is said to have resurrected the errors of Hellenism (the art of which was rejected by Plato). A study of sacred symbolism reveals just how great has been our loss, not only since the Renaissance, but indeed from the end of the thirteenth century onwards.

*

* *

The Gulf between Traditional and Naturalistic Art

This decisive break was the beginning of "European" art, with its succession of well-known styles: "Renaissance", "Baroque", and so on. In later centuries, some individual artists, and some "schools" (such as the Impressionists), opened up certain spiritual possibilities, but they had little lasting influence. There can be no question here of discussing "modern" or "contemporary" art which, with the rarest of exceptions, is simply a matter of degeneration—a degeneration now taken to extremes.

It will probably be agreed that the Renaissance was a revolution, but my apparently uncompromising condemnation of it may surprise, or even shock, readers who have never before encountered this point of view. One can perhaps clarify things by recalling that, whenever there is a breaching of the dykes, there is inevitably a release of energy. Thus, at the time of the Renaissance, there was a tremendous outpouring of genius in many domains. The prevailing spirit seemed to rejoice in the thought that the "shackles of superstition and obscurantism" had been broken.

In the field of painting alone, there were many great Renaissance figures. One example is the early Renaissance Simone Martini, whose paintings display a most touching sweetness and devotion. Nevertheless this was already non-traditional art; the dykes had indeed been broken. The ancient and sacred science of symbolism had gone, and so also the scrupulous respect for the nature of the medium, be it two-dimensional or three-dimensional, be it parchment, canvas, wood, stone, or metal. This having been understood, some indulgence may be shown to a certain Renaissance sensibility, but none to the horrible excesses of the Baroque.

The idea dominating all traditional art is that of unity. The world manifests Divine Unity in multiple mode. "Unity in Multiplicity" (on earth) is the reflection of "Multiplicity in Unity" (*in divinis*).

Titus Burckhardt

CHAPTER 10

INTIMATIONS OF UNITY

Other sheep have I that are not of this fold.

John 10:16

In My Father's house are many mansions.[1]

John 14:2

And Peter opened his mouth and said: Truly I perceive that God shows no partiality, and that anyone in any nation who fears Him, and does what is right, is acceptable to Him.

Acts 10:34-35

Nothing is said unto thee, Mohammed, save what was said to the Messengers before thee.

Koran, *Sūra* "Verses Made Distinct", 41:43

I am neither Christian nor Jew nor Parsi nor Muslim. I am neither of the East nor of the West,

---

[1] This applies not only in Heaven, but also on earth.

neither of the land nor of the sea. . . . I have put
aside duality and have seen that the two worlds
are one. I seek the One, I know the One, I see the
One, I invoke the One. He is the First, He is the
Last, He is the Outward, He is the Inward.

Jalāl ad-Dīn Rūmī

*
* *

In the author's Introduction, reference was made to several
Islamic works of art, both literary and architectural, which
for long have been well-known and much admired in the
West.

Another Islamic treasure much loved in the West was
left unmentioned. I refer to the tales of the celebrated
and inimitable "Mullah Nasruttin" (Nasr ad-Dīn Hoja)!
Humor must not be forgotten. It plays an irreplaceable
role in human relations. It melts hearts, dissolves knots,
abolishes boundaries, and gladdens the soul like few other
things. Humor too is a precious intimation of unity.

CHAPTER 11

A MESSAGE OF HOPE

Throughout this book, there have been repeated references to the unprecedented nature of the times in which we live, and to the ominous and numerous "signs of the times" ("my name is Legion"[1]) which, according to the various religions, signalize the "end times". I have referred to three "falls": the Renaissance, the Enlightenment, and the 1950s and '60s—all recapitulations of the original Fall as related in Genesis. "Ye shall be as gods" (Gen. 3:5) said the serpent; man listened to his words three more times.

Behind all these references, however, lies an attitude of hope and trust in God. We can have faith that, in the end—though it may still be far off—"Truth will prevail". For all the religions, in their respective ways, not only teach the truth, but also provide a means of deliverance; they do not preach despair; on the contrary, they promise salvation.

What is the meaning of it all? The Hindu answer is: "It is the *dharma* of water to flow, of fire to burn, of birds

---

[1] Mark 5:9.

to fly, of fish to swim, and of man to achieve salvation."
The Christian answer is: "Ye shall know the truth, and the
truth shall make you free" (John 8:32). And the Koran,
the last of the great revelations of God to man, says: "All
who believe in God . . . and do righteous deeds—surely
their reward is with their Lord. No fear shall come upon
them, neither shall they grieve" (*Sūra* "The Cow", 2:62).

It is an old message; it is a known message; yet it is one
which today is largely disregarded and forgotten. May this
book act as a reminder!

*
* *

Here is a beautiful summing-up of the spiritual possibilities offered by the "end times" from the pen of Titus
Burckhardt:

> Since nearly all traditional forms of life are now
> destroyed, it is seldom vouchsafed to man to
> engage in a wholly useful and meaningful activity.
> But every loss spells gain: the disappearance of
> traditional forms calls for a trial and a discernment;
> and the confusion in the surrounding world is a
> summons to turn, by-passing all accidents, to the
> essential.[2]

And in the words of Angelus Silesius, in his "Cheru-
binic Wanderer":

---

[2] "What is Conservatism?" in *The Essential Titus Burckhardt*,
ed. William Stoddart (Bloomington, IN: World Wisdom, 2003),
p. 186.

Mensch! Werde wesentlich! Denn, wenn die Welt
  vergeht,
Dann fällt der Zufall ab, das Wesen, das besteht.

Man! Become essentialized! For, when the world
  goes into dissolution,
The accidental disappears, and only the Essence
  remains.

Angelus Silesius

SOURCES

Chapter 2 was first published in *Sacred Web* (Vancouver, Canada), No. 24, n.d.

Chapter 7 was first delivered as a lecture to the Religious Studies Department of the University of South Carolina in March 1993.

Chapter 9 was first published in *Sacred Web* (Vancouver, Canada), No. 28, n.d.

FURTHER READING

Schuon, Frithjof

The Transfiguration of Man. Bloomington, IN: World Wisdom, 1995.

> See especially Part One, "Reflections on Ideological Sentimentalism" and "Usurpations of Religious Feeling".

Castes and Races. Bedfont: Perennial Books, 1981.

Burckhardt, Titus

"What is Conservatism?" In *The Essential Titus Burckhardt.* Bloomington, IN: World Wisdom, 2003.

Sacred Art in East and West. Bloomington, IN: World Wisdom, 2001.

Chartres and the Birth of the Cathedral: Revised. Bloomington, IN: World Wisdom, 2010.

Oldmeadow, Harry

Journeys East: 20ᵗʰ Century Western Encounters with Eastern Religious Traditions. Bloomington, IN: World Wisdom, 2004.

Azevedo, Mateus Soares de

Men of a Single Book: Fundamentalism in Islam, Christianity, and Modern Thought. Bloomington, IN: World Wisdom, 2010.

Perry, Mark

The Mystery of Individuality: Grandeur and Delusion of the Human Condition. Bloomington, IN: World Wisdom, 2012.

Lindbom, Tage

The Myth of Democracy. Grand Rapids, MI: Eerdmans Publishing Company, 1996.

Messinesi, Aristide

"A Craft as a Fountain of Grace and a Means of Spiritual Realization" (on the symbolism of weaving). In *Art and Thought* (a festschrift in honor of Ananda K. Coomaraswamy). London: Luzac, 1947. Also in *Tomorrow* (later *Studies in Comparative Religion*), London, 1965, Vol. 13, No.1.

Lings, Martin

The Eleventh Hour: The Spiritual Crisis of the Modern World in the Light of Tradition and Prophecy. London, UK: Archetype, 2010.

Guénon, René

The Reign of Quantity and the Signs of the Times. Ghent, NY: Sophia Perennis, 2004.

Schimmel, Annemarie

Mystical Dimensions of Islam. Chapil Hill, NC: University of North Carolina Press, 1975.

Hampaté Bâ, Amadou

A Spirit of Tolerance: The Inspiring Life of Tierno Bokar. Bloomington, IN: World Wisdom, 2008.

Fitzgerald, Michael and Judith

The Universal Spirit of Islam: From the Koran and Hadith. Bloomington, IN: World Wisdom, 2006.

Stoddart, William

What do the Religions say about Each Other? Christian Attitudes towards Islam, Islamic Attitudes towards Christianity. San Rafael, CA: Sophia Perennis, 2008.

Invincible Wisdom: Quotations from the Scriptures, Saints, and Sages of All Times and Places. San Rafael, CA: Sophia Perennis, 2008.

Remembering in a World of Forgetting: Thoughts on Tradition and Postmodernism. Bloomington, IN: World Wisdom, 2010.

Outline of Sufism: The Essentials of Islamic Spirituality. Bloomington, IN: World Wisdom, 2012.

BIOGRAPHICAL NOTES

William Stoddart was born in Carstairs, Scotland, lived most of his life in London, England, and now lives in Windsor, Ontario. He studied modern languages, and later medicine, at the universities of Glasgow, Edinburgh, and Dublin. He was a close associate of both Frithjof Schuon and Titus Burckhardt and translated several of their works into English. For many years Stoddart was assistant editor of the British journal *Studies in Comparative Religion*. Pursuing his interests in comparative religion, he has traveled widely in Europe, North Africa, India, Sri Lanka, and Japan. Stoddart's works include *Outline of Hinduism* (1993; 2007 edition titled *Hinduism and Its Spiritual Masters*), *Outline of Buddhism* (1998), *Outline of Sufism: The Essentials of Islamic Spirituality* (2012), *Invincible Wisdom: Quotations from the Scriptures, Saints, and Sages of All Times and Places* (2008), and *What Do the Religions Say About Each Other? Christian Attitudes towards Islam, Islamic Attitudes towards Christianity* (2008). His essential writings were published by World Wisdom as *Remembering in a World of Forgetting: Thoughts on Tradition and Postmodernism* (2008).

Harry Oldmeadow is Coordinator of Religion and Spirituality Studies in the Arts Program, La Trobe University, Bendigo, Australia. A recognized authority on the Perennialist or Traditionalist school of comparative religious thought, his works include *Journeys East: 20th Century Western Encounters with Eastern Religious Traditions* (2004), *The Betrayal of Tradition: Essays on the Spiritual Crisis of Modernity* (2005), *Light from the East: Eastern Wisdom for the Modern West* (2007), *A Christian Pilgrim in India* (2008), *Crossing Religious Frontiers* (2010), and *Frithjof Schuon and the Perennial Philosophy* (2010). Over the last decade he has published extensively in such journals as *Sacred Web* and *Sophia*.

INDEX

Index

For a glossary of all key foreign words used in books published by World Wisdom, including metaphysical terms in English, consult: www.DictionaryofSpiritualTerms.org.
This on-line Dictionary of Spiritual Terms provides extensive definitions, examples, and related terms in other languages.

Other Titles on Islam by World Wisdom

Art of Islam, Language and Meaning: Commemorative Edition,
by Titus Burckhardt, 2009

Christianity/Islam: Perspectives on Esoteric Ecumenism,
by Frithjof Schuon, 2008

Introduction to Sufi Doctrine,
by Titus Burckhardt, 2008

Introduction to Sufism: The Inner Path of Islam,
by Éric Geoffroy, 2010

Introduction to Traditional Islam, Illustrated:
Foundations, Art, and Spirituality,
by Jean-Louis Michon, 2008

Islam, Fundamentalism, and the Betrayal of Tradition:
Essays by Western Muslim Scholars,
edited by Joseph E.B. Lumbard, 2004, 2009

Maintaining the Sacred Center: The Bosnian City of Stolac,
by Rusmir Mahmutćehajić, 2011

Men of a Single Book:
Fundamentalism in Islam, Christianity, and Modern Thought,
by Mateus Soares de Azevedo, 2010

The Mystics of Islam,
by Reynold A. Nicholson, 2002

Outline of Sufism: The Essentials of Islamic Spirituality,
by William Stoddart, 2012

The Path of Muhammad: A Book on Islamic Morals
and Ethics by Imam Birgivi,
interpreted by Shaykh Tosun Bayrak, 2005

Paths to the Heart: Sufism and the Christian East,
edited by James S. Cutsinger, 2003

Paths to Transcendence:
According to Shankara, Ibn Arabi, and Meister Eckhart,
by Reza Shah-Kazemi, 2006

The Sacred Foundations of Justice in Islam:
The Teachings of 'Ali ibn Abi Talib,
edited by M. Ali Lakhani, 2006

A Spirit of Tolerance: The Inspiring Life of Tierno Bokar,
by Amadou Hampaté Bâ, 2008

The Sufi Doctrine of Rumi: Illustrated Edition,
by William C. Chittick, 2005

Sufism: Love and Wisdom,
edited by Jean-Louis Michon and Roger Gaetani, 2006

Sufism: Veil and Quintessence,
by Frithjof Schuon, 2007

Understanding Islam,
by Frithjof Schuon, 2011

Universal Dimensions of Islam: Studies in Comparative Religion,
edited by Patrick Laude, 2010

The Universal Spirit of Islam: From the Koran and Hadith,
edited by Judith and Michael Oren Fitzgerald, 2006

Unveiling the Garden of Love:
Mystical Symbolism in Layla Majnun and Gita Govinda,
by Lalita Sinha, 2008

Wisdom's Journey: Living the Spirit of Islam in the Modern World,
by John Herlihy, 2009